D0506544

Using Drawings
in
Assessment and Therapy

A GUIDE FOR MENTAL HEALTH PROFESSIONALS

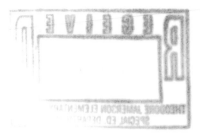
Return to
Counselor Office

Using Drawings
in
Assessment and Therapy

A GUIDE FOR MENTAL HEALTH PROFESSIONALS

by

Gerald D. Oster, Ph.D.

and

Patricia Gould, A.T.R.

BRUNNER/MAZEL, *Publishers* • New York

Library of Congress Cataloging-in-Publication Data

Oster, Gerald D.
  Using Drawings in assessment and therapy.

  Bibliography: p. 181
  Includes index.
  1. Projective techniques. 2. Drawing, Psychology
of. 3. Mental illness – Diagnosis. 4. Art therapy.
5. Group psychotherapy. I. Gould, Patricia,
            II. Title. [DNLM: 1. Art. 2. Art
Therapy – methods. 3. Mental Disorders – diagnosis.
4. Mental Disorders – therapy. 5. Projective
Techniques. WM 45 085u]
RC473.P7077   1987   616.98′1656   86-30958
ISBN 0-87630-458-7 (cloth)
ISBN 0-87630-478-1 (paper)

Published by
BRUNNER/MAZEL, INC.
19 Union Square
New York, New York 10003

MANUFACTURED IN THE UNITED STATES OF AMERICA
10 9 8

Foreword

The modern clinician is faced with an increasing amount of information from empirical studies that have relevance to mental health practice. Biological and epidemiological studies, for example, have provided useful information with direct application to the assessment and treatment of various mental disorders.

In the midst of these scientific advances, it is important to keep in mind that mental health treatment also involves the development and maintenance of a therapeutic relationship between mental health provider and patient/client. This relationship has many subtle aspects and must deal with the patient/client as an individual. This is true regardless of particular diagnosis, treatment approach, or theoretical framework employed. In attempting to establish and maintain this therapeutic relationship, clinicians inevitably encounter difficult-to-treat patients/clients, a good number of whom are relatively nonverbal in therapy. It is in the context of evaluating, establishing relationships with, and treating patients/clients who are relatively nonverbal or who provide only limited information and access to the broader aspects of their personalities through verbal means that various "imaginative," "projective," and "visual" techniques have been developed.

Oster and Gould have written a book that describes how drawings can aid the clinician in the assessment and therapy of various types of patients/ clients, in association with various treatment approaches, and in various stages of therapy. *Using Drawings in Assessment and Therapy* provides valuable clinical insights and helpful strategies, and discusses the use of drawings in mental health from numerous perspectives. It is a real addition to the literature on nonverbal forms of therapy, and it should prove to be a useful resource to clinicians of various backgrounds who wish to broaden and strengthen their knowledge of how drawings can beneficially be used in clinical practice. It is a welcome contribution to the field.

Stewart Gabel, M.D.
Assistant Professor of Psychiatry
Unit Chief, Children's Day Hospital
New York Hospital/Cornell Medical Center
Westchester Division
White Plains, NY

Contents

Preface

The use of drawings has evolved rapidly as an adjunct to aid in accurate diagnoses and enhance the communication and social repertoire of individuals in therapeutic treatment. Because of their brevity, nonthreatening nature, ease of administration, and vast interpretive product, drawings seem to be the most frequent supplement to such projective instruments as the Rorschach and TAT in the everyday tools of the clinical psychologist. Besides their use in assisting the evaluative process, drawings have also been incorporated as vital aids in psychotherapy. Drawings become vehicles for expression of fears, wish fulfillments, and fantasies, as well as concrete expressions of therapeutic goals. They also can be avenues for dealing with frustrations and impulses in the process of developing communication skills to enhance a person's self-worth.

Drawings for evaluation and therapy may include "free" drawings of anything, where the choice of subject matter is completely up to the individual. This type of drawing is primarily used to make projective inferences or to enhance creative expression and may also include more "structured" tasks, in which the clinician imposes more restrictions on the drawings to judge the drawings against some standard or personal reference point.

Examples of this type of instruction may include the copying of designs to assess mental maturity or some kind of organic impairment, in addition to drawings of specific topics at the request of the clinician to elucidate themes of emotional conflicts or to support the goals of therapy.

In this book, drawings and drawing directives are provided to emphasize their usefulness to clinicians involved in the assessment and treatment of individuals, families, and groups in both inpatient and outpatient settings. Case histories are presented to show how the various aspects of drawings can be integrated and applied in clinical practice. Illustrations are used to demonstrate how easy it is to enhance the therapeutic interaction by adding drawings to the clinician's repertoire. Reviews of scoring systems for developmental delays are presented and described as an introduction to the diagnostic process. Also, examples of specific techniques that are commonly used today by clinicians for evaluative purposes are shown. Special chapters, completely illustrated, are devoted to the discussion of family systems theories and group therapy techniques. This book should demonstrate the value of drawings in diagnosis and treatment, and enable clinicians to better use drawings in a more accurate, comprehensive, and meaningful way.

The book is organized into five chapters. The first addresses the historical and developmental aspects of artistic expression and how it became a serious topic of theoretical and practical concern for mental health professionals. This chapter presents the current uses of drawings with regard to the people and settings involved. It is used as an overview of the media of art and why the authors have chosen drawings as the primary focus in this book.

Chapter 2 describes the uses of drawings in the evaluation process. The emphasis is on how drawings have evolved as indicators of developmental and cognitive maturity, as well as personality correlates. This chapter will be especially relevant to clinical psychologists, pediatricians, psychiatrists, art therapists, and others who may find themselves in positions to assess an individual's current functioning. It will also be important to other clinicians who may want to measure an individual's progress in therapy and gather this information by using the different techniques and directives mentioned in this chapter. The chapter also describes various means by which to engage a person in the psychotherapeutic relationship when resistance is confronted. A review of popular techniques used in the diagnostic process is presented, along with case examples and illustrations.

Chapter 3 emphasizes how drawings may be used in individual treatment. A discussion of the therapeutic process precedes examples of techniques and directives that might be used to facilitate greater expressiveness by persons in treatment. This chapter outlines important issues that the mental health professional must consider when introducing drawings into the therapeutic relationship. The chapter also contains many illustrations of various emotional issues that might be encountered when using drawings in therapy. A final view of the therapeutic process details a case illustration.

Chapter 4 presents how art can be combined with family systems theories to better understand the complex dynamics between parents and children. Case examples demonstrate different perceptions of the same family unit, by family members pictorially portraying their view of the family subunits (e.g., dyads and triads, dominant and passive members). These examples show how clearly and succinctly drawings can delineate the organizations and interactions of families better than other, more traditional methods. The chapter also focuses on several theoreticians and modalities of presenting family art evaluations. Special attention is directed to one model (i.e., Haley's strategic model) to illustrate how drawings can be used as an alternative technique by which to generate hypotheses during family evaluations. Other case studies are included to elaborate on the techniques used in family and marital evaluations when drawings are introduced as a means of expression and relating.

Chapter 5 is directed towards the integration of art into group structure and process. Theoretical underpinnings of the functions, purposes, and goals of group treatment are presented, along with an outline of stages that are passed through in group therapy. Considerations in forming groups are discussed, in addition to how to proceed when introducing drawing techniques into the group structure. Many practical points are provided for the group leader who must contend with a variety of difficult clients and situations. The emphasis of this chapter is on sharing; that is, how the group leader can facilitate the idea of sharing space, ideas, and products in enhancing communication.

An appendix is included in the final portion of this book to provide an annotated list of suggested readings and journals. This will allow the interested practitioner or student to pursue a more in-depth study of using drawings as a therapeutic modality. A bibliography is also presented at the end of the book.

This book provides a glimpse into the various uses of drawings as methods or "clinical tools" in assessment and therapy, which hopefully will "whet the appetite" for those clinicians and students who want to pursue ways in which to increase their own repertoire. Drawings can provide a way to release inhibitions and defenses not only from the standpoint of the examinee or patient, but also from the perspective of the mental health professional who must become a participant/observer in the process. The mental health professional, whether physician, psychologist, nurse, social worker, or expressive therapist, brings to each therapeutic encounter his/her own personal judgments and interpretations. This provides the working framework to generate hypotheses, which are needed to explore emotional issues or reveal developmental characteristics. The primary emphasis of this book is not only to share with the mental health professional methods by which to constructively engage a patient in assessment and therapy, but also to attempt to increase communication among the professions.

Early advocates of projective techniques tried to emphasize that empirical evidence is not always essential to justify utilization of a diagnostic procedure (Frank, 1948). And it is true that most methods to be discussed in this book have failed to be considered as reliable or valid measures of personality in a statistical sense. Anne Anastasi, one of the leading experts in the field of psychological assessment, would like mental health professionals to consider these devices as "clinical tools," rather than psychometrically sound instruments or tests, with the distinction being that these devices are "supplementary interviewing aids" (Anastasi, 1982, p. 390). For the purpose of this book we, too, would prefer to make this distinction in order not to dwell on this controversial issue and overlook our main purpose, which is to share the applicability of drawing techniques with the various disciplines that would benefit from them. We take the approach that like any valuable tool, it takes an abundance of clinical experience, combined with a concerted effort to gain knowledge from others familiar in using the particular procedure, to be an effective user of that device. And, of course, it is essential to always use several sources of congruent information before making statements regarding a personality description of an individual.

As this book attempts to establish, drawings not only enhance communication and expression, but also provide pleasure and heighten feelings of mastery and accomplishment in their users. The process of graphic construction may also be useful in the amelioration of psychological distress. The interplay between drawings and treatment can gauge the therapeutic process as well as clarify personality dynamics and uncover underlying conflicts. Drawings do facilitate spontaneity among young children and help the hampered adolescent move beyond his/her personal developmental hurdles. Drawings can also help adults identify recurring themes in their behavior and bring into focus the most salient problem areas in which they may find themselves struggling.

Drawings as seen through the illustrations in this book have the capacity to bring about catharsis of aggressive and hostile feelings into more adaptable modes of expression. Children and adults who have difficulty controlling violent outbursts can be shown alternative strategies that have not been readily apparent to them. Drawings also have the advantage of being client-initiated and client-controlled, which are ego-enhancing actions. The completed drawing, along with the process itself, provides a sense of growth and accomplishment that promotes personal satisfaction and self-worth.

The case examples and illustrations used in this book have been accumulated from many years of training and practice and stem from heterogenous in- and outpatient populations. The names and the presenting symptoms and background information mentioned in this book have all been altered to provide complete anonymity. Also, at times, the pictures have been altered to protect the identity of the client. The pictures chosen for use in this book have been selected only to provide clarity of particular discussions or for intrinsic interest. The combination of case studies and brief vignettes will hopefully stimulate readers to recognize similar situations or problems in their own clinical caseload so that they will want to apply these methods to their daily work.

Acknowledgments

For all their contributions during the writing of this book I (G.D.O.) would like to thank:

My wife, Jo, who was pregnant during the majority of time that this book was being written, and my son, Aaron, whose imminent birth motivated me to finish this project.

Those mental health professionals who have influenced my thinking through the years and who have encouraged my professional development, including those fine individuals in graduate school at Middle Tennessee State University and Virginia Commonwealth University and during my internship year at the Child Psychiatry Center in Philadelphia who helped me in their roles as professors, supervisors, advisors, mentors, colleagues, and most important, friends.

Those mental health professionals during the past several years at the Thomas B. Finan Center in Cumberland, MD, and the Regional Institute for Children and Adolescents (RICA) in Rockville, MD, who constantly sustained me on a daily basis in my roles as staff psychologist, case manager, and primary therapist.

Those clients/patients whom I have engaged in assessment and therapy during the years and who challenged me to use my creative efforts in order to aid their (and my) growth and development.

Brunner/Mazel for their acknowledging a need for this book and to Ann Alhadeff, their Senior Editor, who provided so much energy in her comments to solidify this book.

My parents, family, and personal friends who somehow always provide emotional support for my ideas and adventures.

I (P.G.) would like to thank:

My husband, John, for his support, suggestions, and time spent caring for our child, Austin, while I was writing.

Helen Landgarten, Maxine Junge, and Shirley Riley of Loyola Marymount University, whose clinical training provided me with a strong foundation.

The Thomas B. Finan Center and Community Counseling Associates, both in Cumberland, MD, for facilitating my professional development.

And last, but most immediate, Linda Gantt, whose invaluable supervision broadened my horizons, as well as those I have in turn had the opportunity to supervise, for keeping me "on my toes" when assessing drawings.

Using Drawings in Assessment and Therapy: An Overview

HISTORICAL AND DEVELOPMENTAL ANTECEDENTS TO ART EXPRESSION

Drawings and other artistic creations have always been incorporated into the human condition. Even in primitive times, men and women used etchings and carvings to express feelings and record actions. There is much evidence to suggest that the use of visual forms of art originally served functional purposes rather than merely aesthetic ones (Feder & Feder, 1981). Before humans developed the use of phonetic language they used pictorial symbols to give permanence to their expression of communication. Works of art have long been catalogued in archeological investigations of societal development as examples of how early men and women attempted to produce expressions of ideas and emotions. Thus, drawings must be considered as the basis for elemental communication.

As it is often suggested that individual development reflects the development of the species, so is it that children learn to draw before they can write. One of the earlier analyses and descriptions of children's drawings was completed by Cyril Burt (1921). Based on his personal observation and previous studies, Burt classified the sequences of children's drawings into distinct stages. He suggested children first begin making scribbles at ages 2 and 3. These activities were seen by Burt as purposeless expressions of activity that became more refined and differentiated. By age 4, single lines replace the unorganized scribble. A year or two later, the child, according to Burt, begins to draw crude symbols representing people and animals. During the latency years up to age 10, Burt categorized the child's attempts as descriptive where detail is observed. By age 11, Burt observed the child as able and inclined to copy and trace the works of others. Burt believed that drawings by 11- to 14-year-olds show a deterioration due to possible advances in cognitive and language development and emotional conflicts. The preference for this age group is geometrical forms and decorations rather than human forms. Burt noticed an artistic revival in middle adolescence that leads to more interest in color and form.

Although there is always criticism of any stage theory of development, the majority of investigators do acknowledge discernible differences in drawings during the course of growth. In fact, most researchers and theorists merely refine each of the phases of development. Rhoda Kellogg (1970), who has collected and examined more than a million drawings of young children, has demonstrated that children's drawings develop in an orderly fashion – from certain basic scribbles towards a consistency of symbols. She has shown that instead of meaningless scribblings, children's drawings by age 2 can be differentiated into 20 types of markings. All of these dots, lines and circles display different muscular movement without the aid of visual guidance. Every child, Kellogg believes, can make these markings and those who cannot are somehow disabled. These 20 Basic Scribbles appear to be the foundation of graphic expression and provide a platform for a detailed description of the developmental basis of art.

These and other similar studies have provided mental health professionals with a rich understanding of both the developmental and the psychological aspects of children's drawings. It is especially relevant for the clinician who wants to use drawings as a vehicle for interpretation and diagnosis to recognize that for some age groups abnormal features may be quite the norm. It has been these descriptive studies of children's drawings that have demonstrated the sequences of art development and have laid the foundation for using drawings in such ways as to assess intelligence and personality.

DISCOVERY OF ART BY MENTAL HEALTH PROFESSIONALS

Mental health professionals have also made attempts at understanding the aesthetic experience, explaining the process involved in producing art, analyzing the genius of certain artists, and exploring the meaning of particular pieces of art. Freud (1933), among others, focused an abundance of attention on masterpieces and their creators. Countless volumes have been written on various aspects of the art experience. These works have provided a basis for identifying the complexities of the artistic mind. Both for the artist and the patient the end product is a unique experience of their own struggle to make sense of life. The drawing or other art creation is a very personal statement with elements expressing both conscious and unconscious meanings.

Prior to the turn of the century, mental health professionals focused their attention on the spontaneous writings and drawings of psychotic individuals. This stimulated interest among the various schools of theoretical persuasion and also intrigued laypersons to consider the relationship between the unconscious and creativity. With the advent and appreciation of the psychoanalytic movement, trained psychoanalysts became better able to grasp the symbolism of art products completed by the emotionally disturbed (Kris, 1952).

Freud (1900/1958) hypothesized that symbols represent forgotten memories and are likely to emerge through dreams or art expressions due to intrapsychic stress. The symbol, according to Freud, becomes a disguise for anxiety-laden content and guards the individual from feeling his/her underlying nervousness. Jung (1971) asserted that symbols are a personal experience that is only partially formed. He also emphasized creativity as a primary part in the treatment process and placed special importance on images in the form of archetypes with universal meanings. With both theorists explicating their views on symbols, artistic expression quickly became "food for thought" within the psychoanalytic profession.

Freud's and Jung's explanations of the unconscious processes of the mind gave the users of art for psychotherapeutic purposes a foundation for diagnostic work that followed and paralleled psychoanalysis. Psychotherapists realized that the use of language was not totally adequate for reliving the dream experience and that drawings could provide a partial scene that could not otherwise be described. Thus, with the use of drawings the therapist could directly deal with images as opposed to distorted verbal translations of dream images. Some patients in analysis soon found that it was

5

much easier to construct an image than attempt to describe a dream in words.

Expression through pictures seems much more symbolic and less specific than words. Increased memories and fantasies are likely to result during drawings without the person's awareness of what is being related and with less censored material. The patient can communicate in a vague manner without having to acknowledge that the house in his drawing is not really where he/she lives. This protection from directly confronting emotionally-laden material makes the expression and relating of feelings less anxiety provoking and less likely to produce a defensive posture.

THE PROFESSION OF ART THERAPY

Although there are many clinicians who use drawings to assist in the integration and reintegration of personality, there is clearly a group of professionals who have been specifically trained as art therapists. Art therapists are trained both in symbolic language and in many forms of nonverbal communication (Robbins & Sibley, 1976). Their skills and expertise are now related to the Art Therapist Registered (A.T.R.) by the American Art Therapy Association.

Art therapists look for symbols in the images and attempt to help clients become more cognizant of their inner selves. Art therapists then help their clients to integrate their newly discovered inner selves with their outer realities in the hope that generalizations to the everyday interpersonal behaviors outside the therapeutic experience can occur. Art therapy thus becomes intertwined in enhancing self-expression and understanding.

Like nearly all forms of therapy, art therapy, as a separate discipline, has its roots within the psychoanalytic movement. Within this traditional approach, art therapy was used as an adjunct to psychoanalysis to amplify verbal communication and to provide interpretation of symbolic content derived from the visual images produced by the patients. Art used as a therapeutic modality was pioneered by Margaret Naumburg (1966). She was trained in the tradition of psychoanalysis where free association and interpretation became the main emphasis. She encouraged the use of spontaneous drawings as an ancillary to this technique. Art expression used within this framework became a format in which to elicit and interpret conflictual themes. The value of art therapy was seen in its authentic expression and in its enlargement of communication, where the resulting drawings were part of symbolic speech.

Naumburg was followed in the 1950s by Edith Kramer, who utilized a different approach in art therapy while working exclusively with children (Kramer, 1971). Kramer thought that the art process itself was healing and did not require verbal reflection. She felt that the role of the therapist was to encourage creative production and lend technical assistance and emotional support without allowing diversions into play or fantasy. This variation to art therapy emphasized the therapist as educator and artist rather than as a passive interpreter. This created a polarity in approaches – one emphasizing the creative aspect of the art experience, the other emphasizing the therapeutic insight gained from the art (Wadeson, 1980).

Another major influence in the development of art therapy was Hanna Yaxa Kwiatkowska (1978), who introduced it into family evaluations and family therapy sessions. Kwiatkowska, who worked at the National Institute of Mental Health, discovered that including all family members in an art session was therapeutic both in terms of overall family relations and in strengthening certain components of the family. The family drawings displayed much diagnostic information concerning alliances between family members and how the family members viewed each other in terms of roles and status.

Recently, the humanistic movement in psychology pushed art therapy into the forefront as a primary treatment device, which pays particular attention to the creative product itself. For example, Rhyne (1973) introduced art activities into experiential growth groups, which allowed for an expansion of self-expression, self-perception, and group interactions. Through these pioneering efforts, innovations and variations soon proliferated, and by the 1960s art therapy was recognized as a profession. This created new professional identities for art therapists who soon could be seen in a variety of settings, including both clinical and research facilities.

Today, art therapists can be found in psychiatric hospitals and outpatient clinics performing individual and group psychotherapy as well as aiding in the assessment of individuals and families; in special education programs working with children who are learning disabled, retarded, socially deprived, and/or exhibiting emotional problems; and in nursing homes where art is being used to facilitate the life review process. Art therapists can also be found in drug abuse agencies, college counseling centers, halfway houses, employee assistance programs, and in private practice to mention only a few.

DRAWINGS AS DIAGNOSTIC INDICATORS

There is currently an emphasis on the use of drawings as aids in the assessment process. This burgeoning of interest comes at a time when diagnosticians are feeling stifled by the ineffectiveness of test developers to supply the psychometrically sound procedures needed for understanding of the complex and often subtle problems that they confront in their everyday practices. Even without this quantification, clinicians are holding firm to the belief that drawings can be considered a unique, personal expression of inner experiences which, when used appropriately, can offer clues that are of value both diagnostically and therapeutically. Even though the value of drawings cannot be measured independently from the accumulated knowledge of the clinician, this does not diminish their intrinsic value as aids in working with both impaired and growth-oriented populations. As a keen observer of human behavior, one cannot ignore the sensitivity, intuition, and judgment of the clinician in deciphering messages of communication. Drawings thus combine the entire complex of the clinician and the client and their interaction, which is beyond the scope of predictive methodology.

Drawings have also become an excellent source for measuring current functioning and for expressing present concerns and conflicts during an evaluation. For example, a highly defensive person will usually display his/her lack of spontaneity in drawings by creating monotonous reproductions or by preferring to trace rather than draw (Gumaer, 1984). Characteristics of depressive symptoms in drawings include lessened color, more empty space, greater constrictiveness, disorganization, incompleteness, less meaning, and execution with minimal effort. Drawings by schizophrenics are noteworthy for themes with religious content, and experiences of paranoia are often portrayed by inclusion of eyes, windows, and televisions (Wadeson, 1980). When drawings are interpreted in this manner, they have the capacity to offer many and varied clues to physical and cognitive maturation, certain aspects of personality, and personal perceptions of the world.

As in all interpersonal encounters, it is important that the technique chosen elicits sharing as well as finds personal meaning to the client. This is the essence of any technique that the diagnostician chooses to help in maintaining or increasing rapport with the examinee. Certainly, it is the primary benefit for introducing drawings into any diagnostic situation. Just as dreams were considered by Freud to be the "royal road to the unconscious," so, too, are we and other clinicians who use drawings to aid in the assessment and diagnostic process saying that these concrete mental representations have the advantage of being interpreted in such a manner as to elucidate latent material which is out of current awareness of the individual. It is these representations that can be taken by both the individual and the clinician as symbolic manifestations of inner needs, drives, and impulses that constitute the makeup of the basic personality.

Drawings can also be used as adjunctive interviewing devices in the hands of thoughtful clinicians. Their utility as aids in diagnosis and treatment, of course, lie in proportion to the accumulated knowledge and wisdom of the clinician. Thus, evaluating drawings through psychometric procedures would seem inappropriate (Anastasi, 1982). Even the extensive scoring systems that have been developed appear misleading when used, and their seeming objectivity appears only to be an illusion. The special value of projective instruments remains as clinical procedures. Projective and interviewing procedures offer a large range of information but with low dependability. Furthermore, there is much variability of responses on any one projective instrument from one person to the next. For instance, a person's responses from a series of stories derived from responses on the Thematic Apperception Test (TAT) (Murray, 1943) may provide an abundance of information about his/her aggression, but little regarding achievement orientation, while another set of responses may show creativity but reveal nothing about aggression (Anastasi, 1982). The same can be said of studying and interpreting a series of drawings from various persons. Such lack of uniform responses indicates the low validities discovered when statistical analyses are used to show unidimensional traits across groups of persons. It also again emphasizes the infinite variety of responses that can be derived from viewing responses from psychological test data.

PSYCHOTHERAPEUTIC BENEFITS OF USING DRAWINGS

The process of psychotherapy varies tremendously according to presenting problems and personalities involved. However, there are general features of the process that hold true for most forms of psychotherapy. One of the main aspects of the psychotherapeutic process is to broaden the individual's experiences of expression and relating. This allows the individual to overcome harmful and maladaptive habits or behaviors which are apparently creating intra- and interpersonal discomfort and conflict. Where direct verbal communication is minimal and insight-limited, procedures are needed to provide the clinician with a constructive means to enhance the understanding of underlying conflicts.

Often a single approach directed at helping another person overcome problem areas is ineffective due to the complexities of the human condition. An abundance of therapeutic approaches and theoretical systems of treatment has therefore been created to allow the client as well as the clinician to discover a comfortable working niche. Strategies such as storytelling, play, psychodrama, movement, and dance have all been incorporated into the structure of individual, group, family, and couple therapeutic sessions within distinct approaches (e.g., analytical, gestalt, cognitive-behavioral, family systems). Of all the techniques used in seeking the goals of psychotherapy, drawings seem to accomplish the objectives of developing the individual's expression and ability to relate in the easiest and richest fashion.

For most people, drawings are a less common avenue of expression and therefore less likely to be controlled, allowing more pre- and unconscious material to be revealed. In that drawings provide a platform for individuals to expand their repertoire beyond their usual narrow sphere of senses, unexpected things result, providing a springboard for discussion and learning. Drawings also provide a vehicle for gaining insight into underlying conflicts, ego strength, and character traits. This allows people in treatment to better understand themselves and enhance their appreciation of how they function as individuals and within their family and job/school setting.

Creating a concrete object – that is, drawings – makes it easier to communicate with others than to verbally acknowledge personal feelings, especially if these feelings are frightening. This "objectification" of a feeling allows the person to recognize that the feeling exists and in time the person might be able to take it as part of an internal representation of the self (Wadeson, 1980). The drawing itself also becomes a permanent and helpful record for reviewing the psychotherapeutic process, especially in deciding whether goals have been accomplished and in dealing with termination. The drawing is not subject to lapses of memory. This is particularly crucial over time when repeated themes are noticed. This direct record can also be used for research purposes or can be shared with professional team members for purposes of learning.

DRAWINGS AND OTHER ART MEDIA

We chose to limit this book to the consideration of the value that drawings per se provide to enhance the assessment and therapeutic process. Drawings offer ease of administration, a structured approach to the assessment and therapeutic encounter, and lessen the opportunities for regressive actions by the patient or client that other art materials may produce. Although there certainly is an added benefit to using other art supplies, much more training and experience are required before introducing these materials into the evaluative or therapeutic session. Additionally, much more research and theory have been offered in support of using drawings for diagnosis and therapy than of other methods that are typically used by creative specialists.

For the mental health professional who is not formally trained in the uses of creative media, drawings are generally a safer form of expression. For example, finger painting sometimes becomes too stimulating and, as a less sophisticated form of expression, may lead to regression. This has the potential to complicate the diagnostic or therapeutic session in such a manner that the untrained person may not know how to properly handle the situation. Similarly, the use of clay can often lead to erratic expressions (e.g., beating and pounding), which may appear purposeless to the untrained observer or may in fact be without meaning other than a lack of control (Betensky, 1973).

The kinds of material required for drawings as suggested in this book include pencils, markers, pastels, crayons, and chalks. Pencils generally lend themselves to tighter control, whereas pastels allow greater freedom of expression within a moderate framework of structure during a session, with chalks offering even less control due to smearing. The population with which the clinician is involved will also dictate the choice of media. For example, very young or handicapped individuals may need material that is easier to manipulate (Wadeson, 1980). In that case, the clinician would more likely choose media such as colored markers, which move across the paper easily and do not smear.

A WORD ON COLOR

The significance of color in drawings is beyond the scope of this book, although its use is periodically mentioned in several of the case examples and illustrations. Rorschach, in 1942, was one of the first clinicians to emphasize the relationship between color and emotion. Through the responses to his inkblots, he hypothesized how one's attention to color was central to one's emotional life. For instance, he demonstrated how an absence of color in responding to the inkblots was associated with emotional constriction, whereas many perceptions based on color implied a person who tended to be emotionally volatile. However, an individual's "color ex-

11

perience" remains equivocal (Betensky, 1973). Color can be highly subjective in meaning; therefore, it is especially important for the clinician to pay particular attention to his or her clients' idiosyncratic responses to color.

For the purposes of this book, the mental health professional should be informed of the possible interpretations regarding color when it is used. For instance, the excessive use of the color red is often thought to be associated with the feeling of anger. The continued use of primarily dark colors is usually considered to be a sign of depression. An overabundant use of multiple bright colors may suggest the possibility of manic tendencies. Also, when individuals tend to repeatedly use light, barely visible colors, there is a good possibility that they are attempting to hide their true experience. To reemphasize, however, these are only educated hypotheses gained through clinical experience and do not suggest that this one emotional indicator (i.e., type of color) in a drawing provides the basis for a formal diagnosis.

2

Using Drawings Within the Assessment Process

THE NATURE OF THE ASSESSMENT PROCESS

The purpose of the assessment process is to study an individual's behavior through observation of his/her performance and through a systematic examination of his/her finished product. For the clinician, this evaluative process is usually initiated by a referral source who has specific questions regarding the behavior of an individual. These concerned persons (i.e., parents, teachers, physicians, judges, or other agency personnel) have discovered a problem area(s) in the individual that requires further explanation and possible intervention. Clinicians who routinely do examinations must bring their expertise into this process to translate the identified individual's abilities, dysfunctions, and emotional conflicts into meaningful information, which can then be disseminated to aid the referral source in making more knowledgeable judgments.

The authors of this book are regularly in situations where a physician (usually a psychiatrist or pediatrician), a judge, or another mental health professional has requested answers to specific questions that would clarify his/her decision in recommending treatment services for a particular individual. The nature of assessment thus becomes an attempt at solving these problems that confront the examiner. These questions of behavior are typically viewed as the presenting problems. The following fictional cases are sample illustrations of reasons for referrals.

Case 1

Alice, age 15, the youngest of 11 children, was brought to the attention of the department of social services due to possible sexual abuse by an older brother. During the previous six months, she had stopped attending school and had complained of multiple physical ailments. When placed in a temporary foster home, she made threatening gestures of harming herself and was subsequently sent by the juvenile court to an inpatient unit for an evaluation. The referral questions were concerned with: 1) the severity of this girl's depression; 2) the probability of her making further suicide attempts; 3) her competence to function in everyday academic and social situations; 4) the types of therapeutic interventions required; and 5) the options for placement, if necessary.

Case 2

James, age 6, was referred for a psychological evaluation by his pediatrician due to academic problems in school and angry outbursts in the home. Both parents agreed that James was slower in developing than his older brother and sister, and they had noticed that he seemed to have difficulties hearing and speaking. They described some of his problematic behaviors as having frequent temper tantrums and as being difficult to awaken in the mornings. James was also described as having numerous fears, which extended to animals, clowns, and loud noises. The parents wanted to know what was wrong with James and what kinds of steps they could take to remedy some of these problem behaviors. The referring pediatrician wanted an estimate of James's intellectual abilities and wanted to know whether emotional problems might be hampering his growth and development.

DEVELOPING TOOLS TO ANSWER REFERRAL QUESTIONS

The main point in these examples is that questions are being asked that need immediate attention in regard to diagnoses and to specific recommendations for appropriate intervention strategies within a variety of systems. These personal and social problems require techniques that attempt to determine the nature and extent of the disturbance and yield profiles of functional strengths and weaknesses, so that treatment modalities that would effectively change the troublesome behaviors can be selected and developed. The rationale for assessment then becomes a means to explore the various avenues of treatment. A thorough assessment can provide a baseline of information which establishes a starting point for desired movement by the identified individual and provide the referral source with a plan in which effectiveness can be determined.

For the psychologist, or other health or mental health professional engaged in evaluations, a thorough assessment involves sampling a wide range of an individual's cognitive and emotional resources and attempting to integrate these discrete bits of information with the background information to derive relevant conclusions. These goals require the evaluator to focus on the individual and to gather information directly related to the presenting problems. Once the assessment questions have been clarified from the referral source and assessment goals have been formulated, methods and materials to address these goals must be developed.

Extensive techniques have evolved to help the evaluator in the following: measuring intelligence (e.g., the Wechsler Adult Intelligence Scale-Revised [Wechsler, 1981]); screening for brain impairment (e.g., the Bender Visual-Motor Gestalt Test [Bender, 1938]); gauging educational attainment (e.g., the Wide Range Achievement Test [Jastak & Jastak, 1978]); evaluating severe emotional disturbance (e.g., the Rorschach [Rorschach, 1942]); and addressing descriptions of personality (e.g., the Thematic Apperception Test [Murray, 1943] and the Minnesota Multiphasic Personality Inventory [MMPI] [Hathaway & Meehl, 1951]).

As an aid in this elaborate process, drawings have become an important tool to initiate hypotheses regarding each of these salient areas of concern. Although interpretations of drawings vary based on theoretical orientation, previous research, and personal experience, deductions can be made (with appropriate cautions) and can be viewed within the broader scope of the existing information. It also becomes essential during this process to give significant attention to the individual's personal interpretation of the drawings, especially within the context of his/her developmental stage of life. With this knowledge the clinician can begin providing insight into the conceptual, intellectual, and emotional responses obtained from the patient's performance.

DRAWINGS AS MEASURES OF COGNITIVE MATURATION

From a historical perspective, drawings of the human figure are among the oldest and often the most clinically fascinating of all assessment techniques used with children and adults. The drawing of the human figure was initially developed as a rapid estimate of intellectual maturity by Florence Goodenough (Goodenough, 1926). In this form of assessment, the drawing of a man seemed to be associated with certain developmental milestones in the maturing child and could be viewed in connection with an implicit rule system of growth. For example, a child by the age of 6 could usually construct recognizable drawings of a man. The Draw-A-Man Test soon became one of the most widely used, well-standardized, and validated applications of the drawing technique.

Dale Harris's revision of the Draw-A-Man Test (Goodenough-Harris Drawing Test) has carried on this tradition with an extended and refined scoring system (Harris, 1963). His modification not only added the drawing of a woman and a self-drawing, but also replaced Goodenough's notion of intelligence with his argument that the drawings were an index of conceptual maturity.

Harris delineated three general stages in the age progression of children's drawings. In the initial phase, the focus of the child is centered upon the pleasure experienced in producing marks. Over time, these productions begin taking form and character. This is followed by another stage which includes imitative and reproductive drawings. During this period the child progressively offers increasing differentiation and organization of detail of the human figures. The final general stage is not always obtained in individual development. This is a learned phase where graphic procedures are used based on principles of design and balance. This final stage attempts to demonstrate aesthetically enjoyable results to the individual while communicating to others in a conceptual manner.

Elizabeth Koppitz (1968) has also constructed a system to analyze human figure drawings according to their developmental appearance. She examined drawings to demonstrate the continuum that certain segments of the human figure showed during age progression. Koppitz displays normative data tables for both boys and girls from ages 5 to 12 which describe the number of items "expected," "common," "not unusual," or "exceptional" for the child. The items increase in frequency of occurrence as the age of the child increases, until it becomes a typical feature of most of the human figure drawings at a given age level. Although Koppitz's system does not offer specific values, as does the Goodenough-Harris method of scoring, her system does provide the clinician an opportunity to see whether the child's drawing is common for a child at a particular age.

Koppitz has more recently expanded her research on human figure drawings to include middle school students, aged 11 to 14 (Koppitz, 1984). She demonstrates by numerous tables and illustrations how drawing is no longer a natural pursuit of older children and the details in their human figure drawings do not increase systematically after age 11. This much-needed elaboration of her work again emphasizes the need for researchers to carefully differentiate their sample populations into age groupings when discussing childhood phenomena.

DRAWINGS AS PROJECTIVE TECHNIQUES

Oftentimes, the instructions for requesting drawings can be modified to emphasize the potential of drawings as personality correlates. The rationale behind using drawings in this manner pertains to the development of a sense of self for the child, as well as how the adult views him/herself as an interpersonal being. When drawings are used like this, the examiner is confronting the person with situations that are more unstructured. The examinee must provide meaning for the task from within him/herself via personal experiences. The ambiguity in this use of drawings lies primarily in the minimal direction provided by the examiner. The examinee can then construct whatever is requested in infinite variations as to size, placement, age, and so on of each drawing.

Buck (1948), Machover (1952), and Hammer (1967) have been considered the main proponents of the use of figure drawings as projective instruments. When used in this way, human figure drawings can be analyzed for the appearance of emotional indicators. The emphasis on the drawings then becomes a reflection of the individual's emotional conflicts and attitudes instead of merely a developmental milestone.

These emotional indicators or signs can usually be grouped into three categories. One such grouping is the overall quality of the drawn figure. This relates to such things as line quality (e.g., sketchy or broken), integration of body parts and their proportions, and shading. Another grouping of signs considers the specific features that are typically not seen in human drawings. These include items such as a large or small head, teeth, clinging arms, crossed eyes, cut-off hands or arms, and so forth. The last category of emotional indicators to observe in a human figure drawing is composed of items that are usually expected to be seen. Such body parts as eyes, nose, feet, and neck can be anticipated in drawings completed by latency age children and older. Omissions of these details can be considered important in the final analysis.

Although, like most projective techniques, the quantification of hypotheses and interpretations of drawings has met with discrepant results, the impact of using drawings as projections of the individual's inner experiences has been tremendous (Koppitz, 1968). This popularity among clinicians of using drawings as a useful and nonthreatening approach to gain needed information regarding an individual's conflicts, wish fulfillments, and fantasies has prompted modifications in what is asked to be drawn. These include such alternatives as drawing houses, trees, and families, to name but a few (see sections on common drawing procedures later in this chapter, pp. 19-61).

An assumption is usually made that each requested drawing taps various segments of personaltiy. When a request to draw a house is made, for example, it is usually thought that this will stimulate connections regarding family ties and conflicts surrounding the home life. For children, especially, the emphasis in the construction of this drawing is based on perceptions of parents and siblings. This is also likely to be true of the family drawing where its primary use is to ascertain the outstanding features of the child's perceived status within the family hierarchy. For instance, children who view themselves as having greater significance in the family when compared to siblings will likely place themselves in greater proximity to the parents. In marked contrast, children feeling isolated or different from their siblings might draw themselves off to one side or not participating in a family activity. When a request is made to draw a tree, an assumption is made that the tree reflects deeper and possibly more unconscious feelings about the self. It seems easier in this case to ascribe a greater amount of less desirable personal traits to an inanimate object since it appears more removed from a self-description. The drawing of a person, of course, reflects a more direct expression of real life feelings.

OBSERVATIONS OF BEHAVIOR

The behavior of the examinee during the drawings often yields as much valuable data for the clinician as the actual productions. The observant clinician can make initial judgments regarding such important areas as motor dexterity, dependency needs, tenseness, impulsivity, and insecurities. Additionally, during the evaluative process, the examiner may want to note the changes of tempo, the spontaneity of behavior or comments, and the detail of the drawings to crystallize impressions regarding overall functioning. Certain portions of the examinee's affect are also available to the examiner. For instance, the degree of anger in a voice, the amount of sadness in a face, or the felt anxiety expressed through a hand tremor can all be relevant indicators of inner turmoil. Yet trying to make interpretations based on gesture or expression is far from an accurate assessment of the person, since it is sometimes easy to hide one's feelings and it is only a time-limited sampling of behavior. Thus, there is a need for a wide variety of more objective assessment procedures.

COMMON DRAWING PROCEDURES THAT ELICIT DIAGNOSTIC INFORMATION

The following sections detail the more popular variations of clinical directives for drawings that have been incorporated into the individual evaluations of children and adults. These specific techniques are elaborated upon in conjunction with clinical vignettes. Interpretations are offered to focus on the richness that drawings give to the assessment process and should be taken only as a guide to begin understanding the complexity involved in the presenting dynamics and problems of the particular individual.

Goodenough-Harris Drawing Test

The Goodenough-Harris Drawing Test (Harris, 1963), more commonly known as the Draw-A-Man Test, is used mainly as a screening method by psychologists and pediatricians when a quick estimate of intellectual ability is needed within an evaluation of a school-age child. Of all tests of intelligence, it is probably the most unusual in conception, brevity, and convenience. Its uses have extended to studying children with hearing handicaps, suspected neurological weaknesses, adjustment problems, and character defects.

Intellectual Quotients (IQs) established from this scoring system correspond relatively well with the Stanford-Binet Test and even more closely with the Wechsler Scales. However, the estimated IQ derived from the drawing is usually lower than the scores from these more complete tests of intelligence (Palmer, 1970). Therefore, the Draw-A-Man Test should not be used as a substitute for more comprehensive tests of intelligence and should never be the sole basis for academic placement. It should only be used to select those children who need more careful attention.

The primary objective in this drawing technique is to measure cognitive maturation and is based on Florence Goodenough's early conjectures that an estimate of intellectual development can be formulated from samples of a school-age child's attempts at drawing a man (Goodenough, 1926). Goodenough's scoring system was used without change from its original standardization in 1926 until Dale Harris's revision in 1963. Credits towards an IQ score were earned for inclusion of such features as individual body parts, clothing details, proportion, and perspective. Seventy-three scoreable items were chosen by Harris on the basis of age differentiation, relation to total score on the test, and relation to group intelligence scores.

Directions for administering the drawing by this method are relatively simple. In Harris's revision, the child is typically instructed to draw three figures – a man, a woman, and a self-portrait. This latter directive was primarily included as a projective, although it is rarely used because available research findings were not promising (Harris, 1963). In each of the drawings, the child is asked to construct each figure as completely as possible, that is, more than just the head and shoulders. Unlike methods concerned with personality aspects of the drawing, the Goodenough-Harris scoring system strives for the optimal drawing that the child is capable of producing. Time constraints are not required since the examiner is attempting to assess the child's complete knowledge regarding human body parts.

Drawings by young children are usually very simple. These attempts primarily include a head with few facial features and the remaining body parts stemming from the head. Often, the examiner will see the young child constructing the head and body together as one circular shape. If a child's drawing is merely purposeless or just uncontrolled scribbles, the resulting score would be zero, which is equivalent to 3 years, 0 months in this scoring system. Any drawing that seems to have direction by the child is scored a one and would be equivalent to 3 years, 3 months. Each subsequent point is based on three-month intervals. With ongoing development, the child's drawings become increasingly more heterogenous and precise.

The scoring method provides credit regarding: whether such body parts as the head, trunk, arms, and legs are drawn; whether the arms and legs are attached; whether there are eyes, a nose, a mouth, and hair in the figure; whether there are details of fingers; and whether there are accurate proportions of the features. Tables are provided in the test manual which convert raw scores to standard stores and percentile ranks (Harris, 1963).

Case illustrations.

These simple drawings were completed by a brother and sister, ages 6 and 8, as part of a larger evaluation focusing on possible emotional disturbances precipitated by the violent death of their father. These are examples of how developmental expectations are inherent in the scoring system. Both brother and sister scored within a narrow range of average intellectual functioning (IQs = #99, #101). However, as can be observed in the boy's drawing (see Figure 2-1), his figure is certainly not as complete as the sister's. Hands, feet, and hair are more sophisticated responses that do not usually appear until after age 6. Even though the drawings are remarkably similar, the older sister was able to get additional points in the scoring system by including these features along with a two-dimensional representation of the nose and an indication of shoes (see Figure 2-2).

Draw-A-Person

The Draw-A-Person (D-A-P) test was devised by Karen Machover from her previous experiences with the Goodenough technique for assessing children's intellectual capacities (Machover, 1952). Although numerous art media and techniques had been utilized in searching for salient diagnostic clues up to that time, most attention had focused on drawings of the human figure to explore personality dynamics. Many personal characteristics derived from the drawings of human figures were believed to reflect the person's self-concept. Hypotheses were proposed that the human figure drawing portrayed an unconscious projection of the way the person constructing the drawing actually perceived him/herself.

An emotion, such as hostility, seems to be commonly projected onto drawings. This is done by creating glaring eyes, bared teeth, sneering lips, or even placing weapons in the hands of the drawn person (Hammer, 1967).

My Person

Figure 2-2

Figure 2-1

Poor reality testing may also be viewed in drawings by manifestations of bizarre facial features (e.g., animal faces on human figures), nonhuman, robotlike characters, religious or mysterious symbols on the drawings, or depersonalized, empty facial expressions. Aggressive tendencies are sometimes seen in the use of clawlike hands. Other aspects commonly seen in human figure drawings include concerns regarding sexual identification, portrayals of dominant and inferior persons, and impulses towards rebelliousness and seductiveness.

The Draw-A-Person technique is introduced to the examinee by instructing him/her to simply "draw a person," after paper and pencil are provided. This brief directive, however, is often met with many questions like, "Do I make a stick figure or a whole person or what kind of person?"(Koppitz, 1968). These inquiries are usually best answered with a vague, general statement (e.g., "Make the drawing in any way that you would like"). If the person protests due to personal feelings of incompetence regarding drawings, a reassuring statement such as, "Just do your best," or "I am not interested in how well you draw, rather I am just interested in you drawing a person," or "Whatever you do is all right" will usually suffice.

Upon completion of the initial drawing, the examinee is requested to construct a person of the opposite sex. This is very important in the delineation of sexual identification. According to Machover, the overwhelming majority of persons draw the same sex first from this directive (Machover, 1952). During the drawings, observations are also made regarding the sequence in which different body parts are drawn and other procedural details to begin generating hypotheses about the examinee. At times the examiner may also want the examinee to invent a story about each of the drawn figures to elicit specific characteristics, such as age or personal feelings.

There is a consensus among proponents of the human figure drawing that no one-to-one relationship exists between any specific sign or emotional indicator and a definite personality or trait (Hammer, 1967; Koppitz, 1968; Machover, 1952). Many attempts at researching these variables have shown that anxieties, conflicts, and/or attitudes can be expressed by various means in different people at different points in time. Thus, meaningful diagnoses cannot and should not be made from a single sign; rather, the total drawing, as well as combinations of indicators, must always be considered in analyzing the drawing. In addition, the drawing must be interpreted on the basis of age, maturation, emotional status, social and cultural background, and other relevant history of the individual. An example of an element in a drawing that should be interpreted with caution is sketchiness in the line quality, which is sometimes viewed as an emotional indicator of anxiety. This sketchiness, in fact, seems to increase with age and is normal for most adolescents who almost always demonstrate some degree of anxiety (Koppitz, 1968).

There are, however, some clinically important signs in human figure drawings which consistently differentiate populations in numerous studies on the Draw-A-Person. The following abbreviated list of emotional indicators offers a guideline for viewing these pictures with some assuredness that theoreticians and researchers in this field have concurred on the interpretation for the particular sign.

1) Poor integration of parts in the figure
      Low frustration tolerance and impulsivity
2) Shading
      Anxiety (the greater the shading, the more intense is the felt anxiety)
   (a) Shading of face
         Seriously disturbed, poor self-concept
   (b) Shading of arms
         Aggressive impulses
3) Figure slanting $> 15°$
      Instability, mental imbalance
4) Tiny figure
      Extreme insecurity, withdrawal, depression, feelings of inadequacy
5) Big figures
      Expansiveness, poor inner controls
6) Transparencies
      Immaturity, impulsivity, acting out
7) Teeth
      Aggressiveness (orally related)
8) Short arms
      Tendency to withdraw, turning inward, attempt to inhibit impulses
9) Long arms
      Ambition for achievement or for acquisition, reaching out towards others

10) Big hands
     Acting-out behavior
11) Hand cut off
     Troubled, inadequate
12) Omission of arms
     Guilt over hostility or sexuality
13) Sideways glance
     Suspicion and paranoid tendencies

Case illustrations.

Hannah P., age 14, was court-ordered to an adolescent unit of a state psychiatric hospital for evaluation and treatment. Upon entering the unit, she reportedly was experiencing delusions and hallucinations, that is, stating that demons and devils were entering her body and controlling her thoughts. Prior to her admission, she had been found to be abusing drugs, running away, and truant. She had been hospitalized a year previously after a suicide attempt.

As part of the evaluation process, Hannah was requested to draw a person. From this directive, she quickly constructed a somewhat grotesque person (see Figure 2-3). Although she did not appear psychotic and none of the other portions of the testing supported this diagnosis, Hannah did seem very angry and manipulative. Her impulsive style in completing the picture and the disproportion of body parts suggested poor inner controls and a low frustration tolerance. The inclusion of the teeth is commonly seen with very angry persons. The remaining test data confirmed all these initial hypotheses.

Paul B., age 16, was referred for psychological testing after it had been discovered that he had been sexually abused by an adult leader of his school social club. The original abuse had occurred during an overnight outing. Symptoms that had been relayed to the examiner included increasing agitation with fights in school and a marked withdrawal from social situations. Paul's home life had been unstable, as he had been exposed to frequent moves and three marriages by his mother. His natural father was unknown to him. Before the discovery of the sexual abuse, Paul had been an active member in school and had adequate grades.

Upon a request to draw a person, Paul drew this portrait of a head with minimal consideration given to the inclusion of a body (see Figure 2-4). The outstanding features in this drawing included the controlled anxiety it ex-

25

Figure 2-3

Figure 2-4

pressed (shading and scratchy lines all within clearly demarcated boundaries), the degree of suspiciousness or paranoia Paul was experiencing (the overemphasis on the ear), the fearfulness of thoughts concerning the body (lack of defined shape), and the overall fear he must have felt (the staring, blank eyes). Other portions of the test battery also confirmed the nervousness and distrust that were creating much stress for him.

Draw-A-Person-In-The-Rain

A particularly intriguing modification of the D-A-P is the Draw-A-Person-In-The-Rain. This simple adaptation to the basic instruction of drawing a person has resulted in an impressive array of results. The originators of this variation on the D-A-P (assumed to be either Arnold Abrams or Abraham Amchin [cited in Hammer, 1967]) attempted to design a procedure that offered a perception of the body image when placed within a symbol of an environmental stressor, that is, the rain.

This technique seems to offer useful information to the diagnostician when a concern has been expressed regarding the person's ego strength. Such referral questions as: "How will this person respond to stressful circumstances?" "What kind of personal resources does this person possess to cope with anxiety-provoking environments?" "Is this person able to plan effectively in situations that might be considered anxiety-provoking?" and "What kinds of defenses (e.g., denial, withdrawal) does this person employ when confronted with unpleasant situations?" can all be answered when utilizing this procedure in conjunction with other available test data.

Often individuals will reflect their own perceived helplessness of being "dumped upon" by illustrating a disheveled person with no protective covering (as will be seen in Figure 2-6). This also is likely to represent their underlying minimal self-regard and possible unresolved dependency issues. Persons that construct this kind of drawing neither have the motivation to leave the undesirable circumstances nor are they prepared to face the challenge when left to their own initiatives. Persons who do not feel overwhelmed or who do not panic when confronted with stress will usually draw protective clothing or devices (e.g., an umbrella) and faces of contentment. persons who react unfavorably to the slightest anxiety will most likely portray themselves as panic-stricken without a means of escape.

It is always desirable to make comparisons between this isolated drawing and other person drawings completed during the evaluation, or the other assessment instruments within the test battery. For instance, do suggestions from a drawing reflecting withdrawal tendencies coincide with responses to the Rorschach or TAT, which may indicate a passive style of engaging with other persons? Or does a drawing of a person deteriorate when conditions of stress are introduced? In this latter case, does the person employ an adequate amount of compensatory abilities to present as adequate and only when confronted with external circumstances do the underlying fears reveal themselves? Thus, we get a view of the person in non-stressful versus stressful conditions. Oftentimes a person's disposition towards abnormal reactions is not visible in standard drawings. It is only when an unusual request is made that the existence of any pathological elements is discovered, which of course, is the primary purpose of most projective evaluations.

Case illustrations.

Hank M., age 16, was referred for psychological testing while in a juvenile detention center. The referral was made for placement recommendations considering Hank's history of a violent home situation and explosive outbursts. Results from prior testing indicated above-average intellectual functioning with problems of anxiety and impulse control.

Hank's depiction of a person in the rain was remarkable in its portrayal of the perceived effects of a stressful circumstance (see Figure 2-5). Hank, although drawing the person with some protection – a raincoat and hat – included an umbrella that breaks down in a storm. This lack of complete protection seemed to symbolize his fragile defense system, which the rest of the material in testing also emphasized. It appeared that Hank would indeed, when confronted with stress, have to relieve his anxieties by either running away or displaying destructive outbursts. The house that he drew in the picture seemed to represent for Hank a safe and warm place, which was the focus of many of his wishes. He also indicated through a clear path to the house that is was just down the road, if only he could get out of the storm!

This incredibly sad picture was drawn by Peter L., a 16-year old boy who had been in a residential treatment center for several years (see Figure 2-6). The referral question addressed the extent of his depression and the degree of his reality orientation. He had become increasingly difficult to manage, and placement decisions were to be made based on results of the evaluation. In a recent altercation, Peter had injured someone in a fight after the person had made homosexual advances towards him.

Figure 2-5

Figure 2-6

The drawing resulting from the directive of adding rain to the picture was remarkable for several reasons. First, Peter's initial picture of a person was relatively normal, showing no severe distortions among body parts, whereas in this picture the body became emaciated and the head overly large. This was also poignant in that Peter was markedly obese! This concentration on mental activities was reflected in his Rorschach protocol, which displayed very distant and detached responses to the inkblots. Second, the addition of a stressor (i.e., rain) to the directive allowed Peter to draw an accurate perception of himself when confronted with minimal stress – without outer protection or defenses. Third, the low self-esteem and the intensity of his sadness as exemplified by the facial gesture and poor body image were congruent with Peter's MMPI indicators of depression and sensitivity. From this vivid portrait, a treatment plan was made which altered the focus of treatment and aided this person who was in such distress.

House-Tree-Person

The House-Tree-Person (H-T-P) was developed as an ancillary to intelligence tests that were being constructed during the same time period (Buck, 1948). The H-T-P was originally and is still used as a technique to aid the clinician in gathering data regarding an individual's degree of personality integration, maturity, and efficiency. The discovery that free drawings of these three stimuli provided emotionally constricted persons an avenue for greater freedom of expression also proved to be clinically advantageous.

These three objects (i.e., a house, a tree, and a person) were chosen due to their familiarity to very young children, their acceptance by persons of all ages, and their ability to stimulate a greater fund of associations in comparison to other objects. Besides their use in assessment, drawings of these objects have also been found to be useful as a screening device in group testing for detecting maladjustment, as an evaluative aid for the child entering school, as an appraisal device in screening applicants for employment, and as a research instrument to locate common factors in an identified sample.

A set of instructions is given which specifies that the examinee is requested to draw a house, a tree, and then a person, without any additional comments as to type, size, condition, and so on. The examinee must draw these three objects in any fashion from among the numerous he or she has personally experienced. The ordering of the H-T-P always remains the same because this sequence is viewed as gradually more psychologically difficult, with the tree drawing and the human figure appearing the most likely to produce personal responses (Hammer, 1967).

The house.

The drawing of a house tends to elicit connections regarding the examinee's home and the interpersonal dynamics being experienced within the family setting. The house, it has been theorized, represents the place wherein affection and security are sought. In this manner, a drawing of a chimney emitting smoke is often related to feelings of warmth and affection (DiLeo, 1983). When a request is made to draw a house, the drawing will most likely include only the exterior (DiLeo, 1983). In order to obtain a fuller drawing which would encompass the interior, a direct request from the examiner would probably have to be made.

Interpretations of the house drawings have sometimes been implicated in conflicts of the phallic areas, such as when the chimney is emphasized, and in problems of the oral areas when there are certain kinds of elaborations of the windows (Hammer, 1967). Developmental differences may also be expressed through house drawings. For instance, whereas a child may display attitudes towards parents and siblings in the construction of the house, the married adult will tend to focus on the domestic relationship with his/her spouse. Further, children below age 8 will most likely draw a chimney perpendicular to the slant of the house, whereas the upright chimney demonstrates that the child has surmounted an important cognitive hurdle in his/her development (DiLeo, 1983).

The following indicators provide a limited interpretive guideline for the countless variations that may be observed from the request to draw a house (adapted from Jolles, 1971). Any specific interpretations should only be made in the context of all factors in the combined H-T-P, along with confirmation from the clinical history, presenting problems, and other assessment data.

    1) Details
       (a) Essential (normal drawing)
          At least one door, one window, one wall, a roof, a chimney
       (b) Irrelevant (e.g., shrubs, flowers, walkway)
          Needing to structure environment more completely, which is sometimes associated with feelings of insecurity or needing to exercise control in interpersonal contact

2) Chimney
   Symbol of warm intimate relations and sometimes associated with phallic symbol of significance
   (a) Absence of chimney
       Lacking psychological warmth or conflicts with significant male figures
   (b) Overly large
       Overemphasis on sexual concerns and/or possible exhibitionistic tendencies
   (c) Smoke in much profusion
       Inner tension
3) Door
   (a) Above baseline, without steps
       Interpersonal inaccessibility
   (b) Absence of door
       Extreme difficulty in allowing accessibility to others
   (c) Open
       Strong need to receive warmth from external world
   (d) Very large
       Overly dependent on others
   (e) With lock or hinges
       Defensiveness
4) Fence around house
   Need for emotional protection
5) Gutters
   Suspiciousness
6) Drawn on base of paper
   Basic home or intimate insecurities
7) Perspective, from below
   Either rejection of home or feelings of an unattainable desirable home situation
8) Perspective, from above
   Rejection of home situation
9) Roof
   (a) Unidimensional (single line connecting two walls)
       Unimaginative or emotionally constricted
   (b) Overly large
       Seeks satisfaction in fantasy
10) Shutters

(a) Closed
    Extreme defensiveness and withdrawal
(b) Open
    Ability to make sensitive interpersonal adjustment
11) Walkway
    (a) Very long
        Lessened accessibility
    (b) Narrow at house, broad at end
        Superficially friendly
12) Wall (adequacy of)
    Directly associated to degree of ego strength
13) Window(s)
    (a) Absence of window(s)
        Hostile or withdrawing
    (b) Present on ground, absent from upper story
        Gap between reality and fantasy
    (c) With curtains
        Reserved, controlled
    (d) Bare
        Behavior is mostly blunt and direct

Case illustrations.

Anna O., age 12, was being evaluated for placement in a residential treatment center. She had been adopted by an aunt after having witnessed the death of her mother by her father. Her adjustment after this tragedy had been quite poor despite several interventions. Her household included her sister and three of her aunt's children. She kept the household constantly in an uproar with threats of aggression towards her cousins and suicide gestures.

When requested to draw a house as part of the test battery, Anna hastily drew the above drawing (see Figure 2-7). Besides her impulsive and uncaring style, Anna also represented several relevant emotional qualities in the drawing which were later substantiated in other portions of the evaluation. The long walkway attached to the lower left base of the paper seemed to indicate her need for structure in her environment and at least her ambivalence towards emotional accessibility. The bare windows appeared to point to her direct and blunt interpersonal approach. Also, the single line stemming from the chimney possibly suggested the lack of emotional nurturance which she perceived existed in the household.

35

John K., age 14, was being evaluated to assess his intellectual and emotional status. This evaluation was conducted to assist the treatment team in developing appropriate strategies for therapeutic planning and aftercare. For the past year he had been living with his father and only recently had moved into the home of his mother and her new husband. At the time of testing, he did not seem to have had the opportunity to work through his parents' divorce and had not accepted his stepfather as a person of supportive strength. His poor adjustment since his parents' divorce in-

Figure 2-7

cluded problems in school attendance, delinquency surrounding stealing and fighting, and displays of temper outbursts. During the initial part of the evaluation, he was requested to draw a house to provide a basis for understanding his particular home situation.

In this drawing, John drew a very detailed house, but from a perspective from above (see Figure 2-8). As mentioned in the list of emotional indicators for the house, a drawing from this perspective usually represents an attempt at completely rejecting the home situation. Certainly, this was true for John, who was not prepared to reenter his mother's home.

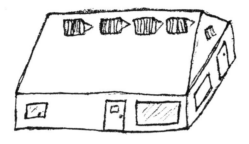

Figure 2-8

The tree.

The drawing of the tree is believed to be associated with one's life role and one's capabilities in obtaining rewards from the environment. Generally, tree drawings have been considered especially rich in providing insights concerning "life content," that is, displaying accurate biographical situations and/or offering personal characteristics of the person being examined.

The tree seems to reflect longstanding, unconscious feelings towards the self and these feelings tend to reside at a more basic, primitive level. The tree also appears to be an easier object than the person or house on which to project negative self-feelings and is one step removed from the "closer-to-home" drawing of a person.

Besides Buck's description and interpretation of tree drawings in his H-T-P manual, two other systems have been developed that have focused on the tree as a sole diagnostic entity, offering lengthy descriptions and details concerning its interpretive value (Bolander, 1977; Koch, 1952). The reader should refer to these books for a fuller understanding of the use of tree drawings as projective instruments.

The following signs or marks that might appear on a tree drawing are just a tiny sample of possible interpretations but do give the reader an initial guide for exploring emotional hypotheses related to the examinee.

1) Extremely large tree
   Aggressive tendencies
2) Tiny tree
   Inferior, feelings of insignificance
3) Faint lines
   Feelings of inadequacy, indecisiveness
4) Tree composed of just two lines for trunk and looped crown
   Impulsive, variable
5) Exaggerated emphasis on trunk
   Emotional immaturity
6) Exaggerated emphasis on crown
   Inhibited emotionally, analytical
7) Exaggerated emphasis on roots
   Emotional responses shallow, reasoning limited
8) Scar, knothole, broken branch
   Associated with trauma, e.g., accident, illness, rape (time determination in relation to length of tree)
9) No groundline
   Vulnerable to stress
10) Groundline present, no roots
   Repressed emotions
11) Shading, excessively dark or reinforced
   Hostile defenses or aggressive behaviors
12) Fine, broken lines
   Overt anxiety
13) Knotholes
   Sexual symbolism
   (a) Small or diamond-shaped
      Related to vagina
   (b) Small and simple
      Sexual assault or initial sexual experience
   (c) Outline reinforced
      Shock impact greater
   (d) Circles inside
      Experience in past and "healing"

(e) Blackened
    Shame associated with experience
(f) Large
    Preoccupation with procreation
(g) Small animal inside
    Ambivalence surrounding childbearing

Case illustrations.

Jennifer R., age 8, was referred for psychological testing at an outpatient child psychiatric center due to a continued progressive decline in her educational achievement. There were also behavioral concerns noted in her referral including fighting with a younger sibling, stealing, and enuresis. Indications of possible physical or sexual abuse were noted on the intake form. During the initial portion of the evaluation, Jennifer was asked to draw a house, a tree, and a person.

As a result of this directive, she drew a tree which seemed to reveal much of her underlying upheaval (see Figure 2-9). Some of the outstanding features of this drawing, which were used for hypotheses concerning her present condition, included: 1) heavily reinforced lines of the bark and shading to represent hostile and aggressive defensiveness; 2) scribbling to represent anxiety; 3) branch structure abruptly flattened at top to represent an attempt to reject or deny painful fantasy life; 4) overemphasis on roots entering ground to represent insecurity; and 5) blackened knothole to represent a considerable amount of shame associated with trauma, which appears to be recent. From these emotional indicators and other supporting test data, it seemed apparent that a recent trauma had happened to this girl. This was later confirmed by a further investigation by protective service caseworkers, who discovered incest to be occurring in the family.

Lynne S., age 11, had entered an evaluation unit of a state psychiatric hospital due to increasingly out-of-control behaviors including fighting, temper outbursts, truancy, and breaking and entering into neighbors' houses. When asked to draw a tree, Lynne quickly drew a somewhat well-balanced tree (see Figure 2-10a). Although there were some minor emotional indicators of anxiety (inconsistent bark), impulsive, aimless behavior (hidden branches), and expansiveness of behavior (large tree), overall the tree indicated a rather well-balanced figure considering Lynne's background (isolated, country existence) and presenting problems. Soon thereafter, Lynne spontaneously turned the paper over and suddenly remarked that she

My Tree

Figure 2-9

thought the examiner had asked her to draw a tree as others would and said that it was not her tree. With this she hastily constructed a tree that was strikingly different and said that this was her way of drawing trees (see Figure 2-10b). As can be observed in this drawing, the tree appears much more imbalanced and impoverished in contrast, which seemed more similar to her emotional state. The broken or dead branches usually reflect the presence of past physical trauma and the loss of satisfaction in life (both being readily apparent in her life). Also, the wavy trunk seemed a truer picture of her regressive and impulsive behavior than did the previous drawing. Lynne, because of her personal awareness and ability to respond to external controls and limits, was able to return to the community to live in a structured group home with counseling provided.

The person.

The drawing of a person seems to stimulate conscious feelings regarding bodily image and self-concept, both physically and psychologically. For example, feelings of inadequacy may be represented by tiny drawings or dangling arms. The drawing of a person may also be seen as arousing emotions concerning interpersonal relationships and may also tend to elicit feelings towards an ideal self. Of the three H-T-P drawings, the person is the most difficult to draw and the most likely to be rejected by persons who fear failure; thus, a request to complete the drawing needs the most encouragement from the examiner. Since the drawing of a person has historically been the most discussed of the three items and has several variations of scoring (see preceding sections on the Goodenough-Harris Drawing Test and Machover Draw-A-Person Test), it will not be elaborated upon here. However, the following signs can be added to those given in the other sections to provide a fuller awareness of possible emotional indicators (adapted from Jolles, 1971).

1) Arms
   Used to change or control surrounding environment
   (a) Folded over chest
       Hostile or suspicious
   (b) Held behind back
       Wanting to control anger, interpersonal reluctance
   (c) Omitted
       Inadequacy, helplessness

41

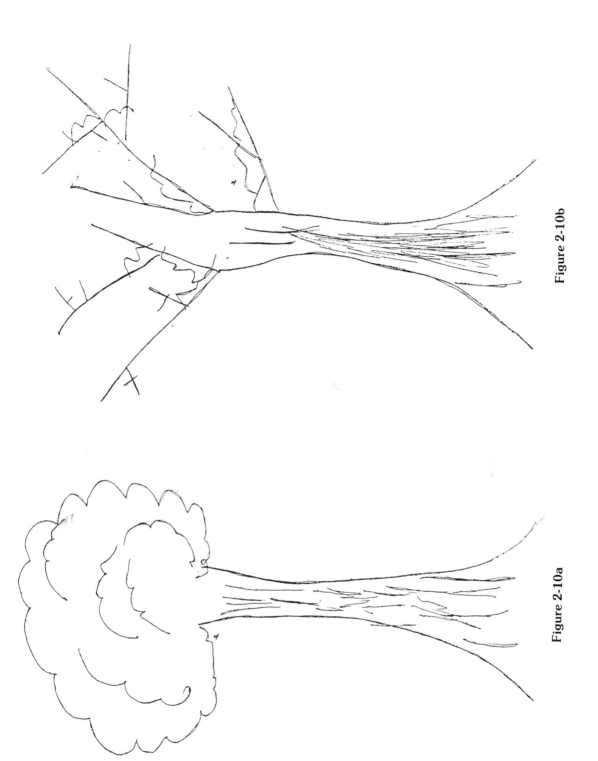

Figure 2-10b

Figure 2-10a

2) Feet

   Degree of interpersonal mobility

   (a) Long

   Striving for security or virility

   (b) Tiny

   Dependency, blunted feelings

   (c) Omitted

   Lack of independence

3) Fingers

   (a) Long and spikeline

   Aggressive, hostile

   (b) Enclosed by loop or single dimension

   Wish to suppress aggressive impulse

4) Head

   (a) Large

   Preoccupation with fantasy life, focus on mental life

   (b) Small

   Obsessive-compulsive, intellectual inadequacy

   (c) Back to viewer

   Paranoid or schizoid tendencies

5) Legs

   (a) Absent

   Constricted, possible castration anxiety

   (b) Size difference

   Mixed feelings regarding independence

   (c) Long

   Striving for autonomy

   (d) Short

   Emotional immobility

6) Mouth

   (a) Overly emphasized

   Immaturity, oral-aggressive

   (b) Very large

   Orally erotic

7) Shoulders

   (a) Unequal

   Emotionally unstable

   (b) Large

   Preoccupied with the perceived need for strength

   (c) Squared

   Overly defended, hostile towards others

Case illustrations.

The two following examples display combined House-Tree-Persons which were given with the instruction to place all three figures on a single page. This directive provides continuity among the figures and also offers the opportunity to elaborate on a story when postinterviews are given.

William R., age 9, was brought to an outpatient mental health center by his parents on the recommendation of his elementary school teacher. He lived in a household consisting of his father (a shipper), his mother (a full-time housewife), two sisters, ages 7 and 1, and two brothers, ages 5 and 3. Presenting problems included behavioral difficulties both at home and at school. William's problem behaviors were lying, stealing and experiencing considerable conflict with his siblings. At school, he had been suspended on several occasions for fighting. There was also a report of physical abuse in the home.

In his attempt at a House-Tree-Person, William's most significant figure was the person, alluding to his self-absorption (see Figure 2-11). The emphasis on the mouth with its jagged teeth suggested much hostility and an oral-aggressive style. When hats are included, as in this case, it is usually indicative of a person who is exerting much energy to control angry feelings to reduce the fear of becoming overwhelmed by them. Also in this figure, reinforced marks were placed around the belt, which appeared suggestive of sexual concerns. The house and tree seemed bare and controlled with little overt signs of disturbance. The swing on the porch (right side) looked more like a beam to indicate the house was beginning to crumble. However, the story William told about the figures seemed overly docile as he remained guarded and denied many of his angry feelings throughout the evaluation. As a result of the assessment process, William and his family were able to enter into a therapeutic relationship with a family therapist.

Charles K., age 15, was admitted to a state psychiatric facility for verbal and suicide threats, delusional experiences, running away, and killing a cat in a halfway house. He was perceived as being preoccupied with violence and retaliation and as being chronically depressed. Before being taken out of his home, he had been arrested for breaking and entering and for possession of several guns.

Charles's construction of the House-Tree-Person was remarkable for its heavy emphasis on needs for control, apparent suspiciousness and paranoid tendencies, and its overt aggression (see Figure 2-12). Charles drew the house with special attention to heavy outlines around the exterior,

44

Figure 2-11

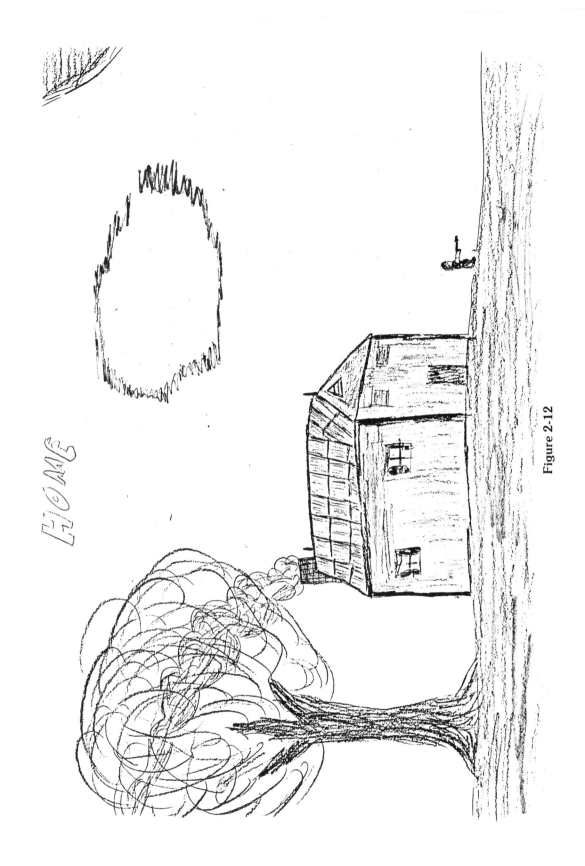

Figure 2-12

including a lightning rod (need for structure and control), shading (anxiety), elaborate smoke profusion from chimney (anger within), emphasis on roof (attempt to control inner fantasy), and the inclusion of a peephole in the door and shades on the window (both signs of suspiciousness and paranoia). The drawing of the tree, in contrast, suggested a much healthier personality. Only emotional indicators of anxiety and compulsive behavior were readily apparent. Charles first approached the drawing of the person by making it very large, indicating some grandiose quality in his self-perception. Soon, however, he erased the figure and made it quite small, suggesting underlying feelings of inadequacy. The figure was protecting his home by firing a gun at intruders. He was able to relate the drawing to what had happened to him before he had been removed from his home.

With the information provided by the H-T-P, along with concurrent knowledge derived from other evaluations performed by the multidiscipline treatment team members, Charles was detained in the hospital and provided with a variety of therapeutic modalities to enhance his self-esteem and reality testing.

Draw-A-Family

The Draw-A-Family or Family Drawing Technique is an elaboration on using person drawings as projective indicators of personality. This informative device was initially suggested by Appel (1931) and later elaborated upon by Wolff (1942). Its tremendous popularity most likely parallels the current therapeutic emphasis on family structure and family intervention. Its brevity, along with the wealth of information gained from its administration, makes it an attractive addition to the arsenal of examining tools used by both health and mental health professionals.

The instructions for this informative technique are minimal. The examiner provides the examinee with pencil and paper and asks him/her to "draw a picture of your whole family" (Harris, 1963). If the person does not offer the names of the family members, he/she is asked to identify them afterwards. The resulting drawings tend to reveal a person's attitude towards family members and his/her perception of family roles. Family relationships are often expressed by the relative size and placement of the figures and by substitutions or exaggerations of the family members. It is sometimes seen that the examinee will omit him/herself from the family drawing, which is usually a reflection of feelings of rejection. This is particularly demonstrated in family drawings by adopted children, especially during their adolescent years when identity concerns become focused (DiLeo, 1983).

Another useful modification to the family drawing is found in the Kinetic Family Drawing (K-F-D) (Burns & Kaufman, 1970), which adds the drawing directive, "Do something (an activity) together." This variation also asks the individual to include him/herself and is usually given after the first family drawing so as not to contaminate the possibility that the individual will omit him/herself. This latter addition often produces a reaction like, "We don't do anything together" (which is certainly salient information in the gathering of initial hypotheses concerning familial interaction, especially in children). Although this directive is very pertinent when used with children, it also stimulates perceptions of previous years as a child when used with adults and brings forth memories of past family experiences and interrelationships.

Many times individuals will draw their families engaged in a very passive posture (e.g., watching television or a movie), which suggests to the clinician a possible lack of interpersonal communication. Another common response when using the kinetic family drawing technique results in pictures reflecting scenes from the dinner table. Here the examinee might place the parents at opposite ends of a long table (displaying their perceived emotional distance from one another) or might even place him/herself at one end (attesting to the competition that he/she probably experiences). Whether the dinner table is full or bare might address the examinee's worries regarding living in a bleak environment or concerns regarding the amount of emotional nurturance.

Other factors to be ascertained from the drawings include trying to assess such important dynamics as those between parent(s) and examinee and between siblings and examinee. Clues to these dynamics might be: 1) whether the examinee draws him/herself in proximity to the parents to express perceived status among the siblings or to show feelings of rejection; 2) whether he/she omits siblings partially or entirely to indicate a symbolic means to eliminate competition; 3) whether the family is drawn in accurate proportions, which when discrepant by making a child or adult much taller demonstrates perceived dominance or ineffectiveness; and 4) whether the examinee is included in the drawing (an attempt to demonstrate a feeling of not belonging). Another clinical sign to notice from the drawing is the different expressions of the parents if they can be ascertained. Such indicators as whether the examinee perceives one parent to be harsh, one to be gentle, or one to be more supportive are all important areas to pursue during the rest of the examination to give direction to future therapeutic planning.

Case illustrations.

The drawings in Figures 2-13a and 2-13b were done by an 11-year-old boy, Jake O., who was being seen as part of a child mediation case by a psychologist. The case involved a joint custody disagreement in which Jake's mother wanted to spend more time with him. Prior to entering into a court contest, the parents wanted to try to settle their dispute without the expense of a trial. When the psychologist became involved in this process, Jake was living primarily with his father and stepmother. The mother had only recently remarried.

As part of the evaluation, Jake was requested to make two drawings – one drawing of him involved with each family "doing something together." In the first drawing (see Figure 2-13a), Jake drew himself sitting around the television with the other members of the family. This passive picture suggested little interaction among the family members. It was interesting to note that Jake placed himself furthest away from his father as there seemed to be some tension between the two. He also indicated that he was still unsure of the role his stepmother played in his perceptions, as he added a question mark next to her name (Kate?). In his second picture, he portrayed himself sitting at a dinner table with his mother and stepfather (see Figure 2-13b). This picture is relevant in its depiction of more interpersonal interaction. The circular table even seemed to enhance the individuals' emotional closeness. These pictures were certainly enlightening to the examiner and proved to be an accurate reflection of the family dynamics within each household. They provided much valuable information for further discussion of Jake's involvement in each of his two families.

Jane R., age 15, was referred to a private physician due to chronic depression and drug abuse. She had been suspended from her middle school for a high frequency of unexcused absences. As part of the medical work-up, Jane was asked to construct a family drawing that included herself. The resulting drawing showed minimal communication among the various family members (see Figure 2-14). In fact, everyone seemed very withdrawn and invested in his/her own separate activities. The father was portrayed as watching television and drinking beer. The mother was studying and reading a book. Finally, Jane was lying down with both stereo speakers on either side of her head. Obviously she did not want her parents to interact with her. Alerted that this appeared to be a problem most likely to be resolved by family therapy, the physician referred Jane and her family to a mental health center specializing in family therapy.

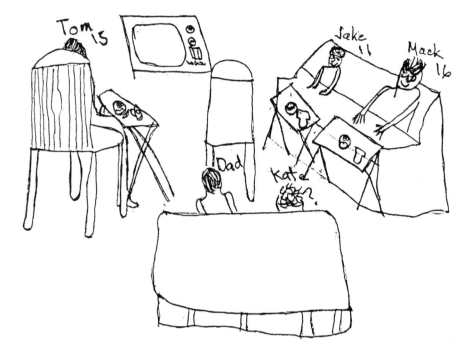

Figure 2-13a

Figure 2-13b

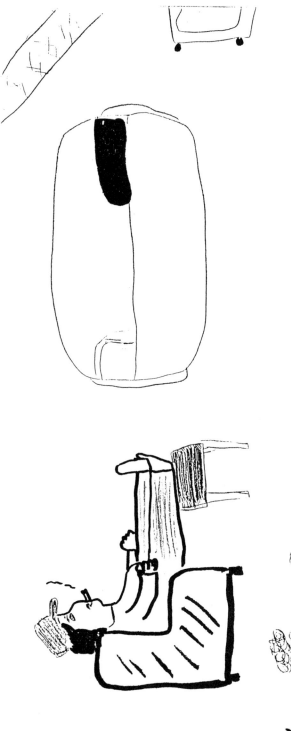

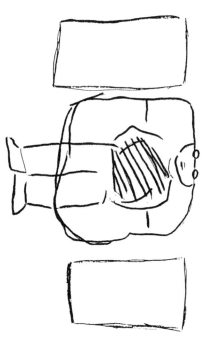

Figure 2-14

This kinetic family drawing shows a family that had been divided (both figuratively and literally) (see Figure 2-15). The two people on the left are the two sons in the family. The brother on the right had already left home, while the younger brother, who drew this picture, had been recently hospitalized for out-of-control behaviors. This younger brother also was completing school and was soon to leave home. The upraised rackets seemed to have signified the two brother's independence from the family or possibly was a sign of their aggressiveness. On the other side of the net was the father, sister, and mother (the furthest from the boys). It seemed that the sister was in a position to intervene between mother and father (placed between two parents). From this drawing many hypotheses concerning the family's difficulties were surmised and confirming evidence was sought during the remaining part of the interview and evaluation.

Free Drawings

Free drawings or free association drawings are usually requested at the beginning of a series of drawings. They can also be of value when the persons being tested are unusually nervous about trying to pictorially express themselves. Most individuals, especially children, would prefer to draw whatever they want to, rather than have someone impose structure on them. In this manner, they are ordering the world in the way they want it and are more likely to cooperate with future instruction. When individuals are drawing freely and without direction, they are expressing a part of their own personality and perceptions. The experience becomes a time for independent thought and action, which is a primary goal of therapeutic intervention. In the process, these individuals are releasing their own feelings and attitudes, which may have been inhibited or unavailable.

The usual directive given to individuals when using this technique is a request to "draw anything" and to "verbalize whatever thoughts and feelings" they might be experiencing during the process. This instruction is used in an attempt to reduce anxiety and counteract the situation where they think that they cannot draw. The free drawing increases the opportunity for persons being evaluated to open up to the examiner and enhances the possibility to demonstrate impulsive actions, reveal fantasies, or provide freer associations to conflictual areas, which are all pertinent to the gathering of data for diagnostic purposes.

One of the earlier users of free drawings was Margaret Naumburg (1966), a pioneer in using art as a serious therapeutic tool. She relied heavily on the spontaneous drawings of her clients and how they associated to their pictures. The resulting verbal associations to a free drawing provide a rich fund of relevant information for the diagnostician who is trying to rule out serious psychopathology and who is attempting to identify strengths and weaknesses of the examinee. The art product and the individual's associations to the finished work give the examiner some glimpses into a very personal experience. It is the addition of sponteanous verbal communication that makes this technique an immensely valuable and enlightening tool.

Case illustrations.

When asked to make a free drawing during the first part of a psychological evaluation, Jim C., age 16, drew a flag with the word "FREEDOM" on it (see Figure 2-16). This was especially appropriate for Jim who presented himself as rebellious and independent. The drawing also appeared to signify the dilemma he was facing, as his parents had recently divorced and he was not adjusting to either of their households. Similar to the drawing, his emotional profile from an MMPI administration portrayed Jim as being generally defiant of authority figures, argumentative, and vulnerable to per-

Figure 2-15

ceived threats. Other youths with like profiles tended to undercontrol their impulses and act without sufficient thinking and deliberation. With agreement from both these projective and objective tests, the psychologist was able to substantiate his recommendations for continued treatment.

A 36-year-old woman was referred to an outpatient psychiatric clinic for an evaluation due to an episode of depression. This woman, who was an artist, had recently discovered that her mother had been diagnosed as having cancer. As part of an introductory session with a psychiatrist she was requested to make a drawing of anything she desired (see Figure 2-17). Her free-floating drawing seemed to indicate her active denial of expressed feelings. The empty quality of the drawing also suggested to the psychiatrist some possibility of underlying depression. In later therapeutic sessions, interpretations of similar drawings were made and the woman's artwork began to show more accurately her feelings of sadness and anger.

The Scribble

The "scribble" technique, described by Florence Cane (1951), is viewed as a valuable tool for establishing rapport with adolescents and adults, and to some extent, with preadolescents (Kramer, 1971). It seems to be an entertaining, nonthreatening method to help individuals express out-

Figure 2-16

54

wardly those portions of their inner selves that they are reluctant to share. The original procedure had patients first use their entire bodies to draw in the air with wide and rhythmic movements. Then, after a freedom of motion was experienced, the patient, with eyes closed, would transfer this motion onto a sheet of paper. The idea of the body exercise was to effectively free the individual in overcoming inhibitions, allowing him/her to make less constricted scribbles on the paper. The authors of this book have discovered that an entire series of warm-up exercises is desirable before presenting the directive of drawing the scribble. This seems to allow a greater degree of dexterity and creates an enjoyable, relaxed interaction between the examiner and the examinee.

The next step, after the scribble is completed on the paper, is to

FLIGHT — LIGHT AND AIRY — FLOATING - FREE

Figure 2-17

examine it from all angles until forms are found that suggest a picture. The picture is then completed by using those lines that match the mental image and removing others. The final product bears minimal resemblance to the original lines on the paper. Some individuals will find more than one picture, while others will outline and color in a larger, more comprehensive picture. The process usually starts the person talking about the various forms and sometimes a spontaneous story will result.

This method of breaking down inhibitions serves several important functions. First, the idea of departing from a simple drawing request into directing patients to incorporate their entire bodies in exercises provides them with novel experiences which stimulate free associations. This is especially relevant for patients who may have gone through routine evaluations prior to entering the current testing session. Second, patients are encouraged to become more childish and possibly produce novel or forbidden movements which increases spontaneity or allows freer expression of moods. Third, the act of discovering an image in the scribble increases the chance of encouraging latent fantasies that might be projected onto the random marks. The resulting image is thus likely to represent more personal concerns. Finally, the completed idea constitutes a creative process and a nonverbal, artistic communication, which fulfills an important aspect of using drawings in assessment batteries.

Case illustrations.

Janet C., 15 years old, was voluntarily admitted to an adolescent inpatient unit due to sporadic violent outbursts and displays of psychotic symptoms. She had always found school rather difficult and had a history of academic problems and a documented learning disability. A referral was made for a comprehensive psychological evaluation by the unit psychiatrist. Because Janet seemed unusually tense and anxious during the initial phase of the session, the testing psychologist used a series of warm-up exercises and a scribble drawing to create a more responsive atmosphere. Janet used this opportunity to relax and completed the scribble shown in Figure 2-18. Commensurate with her presenting displays of temper, she chose to project onto her scribble a fist to represent her constant anger. This was certainly a main theme that was present throughout the entire evaluation. With the information that Janet preferred to act on her anger, and that focused relaxation methods could help her control her feelings, the psychologist recommended to the treatment team to include her in movement therapy

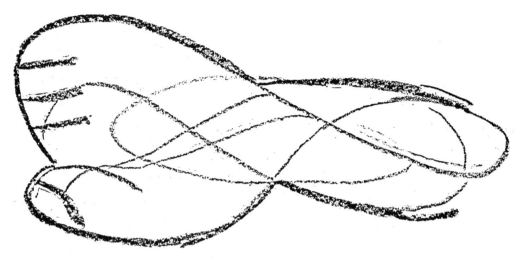

Figure 2-18

and psychodrama to teach her new modalities in which she could channel her energies.

The scribble drawing in Figure 2-19 was constructed by a 36-year-old woman who had been hospitalized with the diagnosis of paranoid schizophrenia. As part of an art evaluation she made a turtle out of her scribble drawing. She interpreted her drawing as representing her tendency to do things slowly and to procrastinate. She also discussed it as a portrayal of her vulnerability and her need for isolation. She, like the turtle, often withdrew into her protective shell when feeling fearful or stressed. Her primary therapist, a social worker, who was working in co-therapy with the art therapist, was able to use the turtle as a metaphor in helping this woman "come out of her shell."

Draw-A-Story Game

Every examiner or therapist has at one time or another been confronted with individuals who are resistant to drawings. At times children will be extremely anxious, or adolescents hostile and oppositional, or adults unreceptive to engaging in an activity they feel is not relevant to their concerns. Resistance in this form is not just a way to defend oneself against painful self-disclosure, but seems to be an unwillingness or hesitancy to become involved with another person. It is from these frustrating experiences of

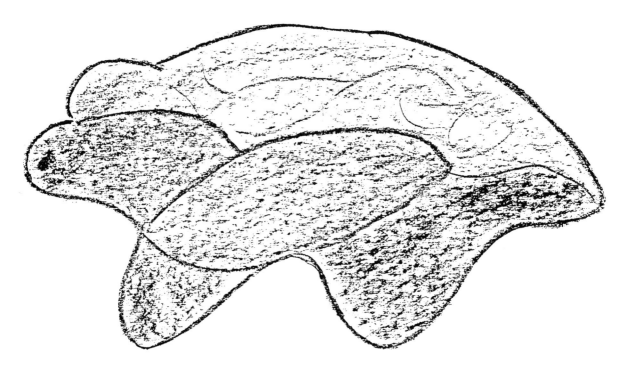

Figure 2-19

working with resistant individuals that other variations of approaching the reluctant examinee have been offered by clinicians to help work through these times of "being stuck" (Gardner, 1975).

One such technique, which combines elements of drawing and storytelling, has been described in *The Arts in Psychotherapy*, a professional journal for clinicians (Gabel, 1984). The creator of this technique, Stewart Gabel, a pediatrician and psychiatrist, combined ideas gained from procedures developed by child psychiatrists Donald Winnicott (1971) and Richard Gardner (1975), and evolved them into an engaging technique called the Draw-A-Story game. The "game" is most helpful in working with children and adolescents who are unable or who seem reluctant to interact fully in diagnostic or initial therapy sessions. Although developed for use with children, the Draw-A-Story game could easily be adapted for lower functioning adults.

In borrowing from the "Squiggle Game" by Winnicott where the child and clinician alternately draw squiggly marks and turn them into something therapeutically meaningful, Gabel offered a more structured approach to reaching unconscious or emotionally avoided material. Gabel also added a modification to the "mutual storytelling techniques," which Gardner has used so credibly in his work.

In this interactional game (i.e., the Draw-A-Story game), the examiner or therapist first draws a simple line on the paper and directs the individual to elaborate on the mark in order to make a picture. It is after the product is finished that questions like "Who is that?" or "What's going on there?" can be introduced to engage the individual in more prolonged discussion. After this initial phase, the individual is then asked to make the first mark on another sheet of paper. The examiner then incorporates this mark into a picture, which is a progression of the examinee's picture, and initiates a sequence of pictures that eventually becomes a more complete story. This alternating process continues to maximize the interaction and maintain rapport with the client, as well as to provide salient diagnostic material and to add to the client's self-awareness.

When a series of drawings with an accompanying story has been completed, the drawings can be reviewed to reemphasize the moral or lesson to be learned. At that time it is also valuable to suggest to the child that he/she create other outcomes to the story which perhaps would be more satisfying. In this manner, the examiner or therapist is adding to the child's awareness of alternatives to feelings and actions. According to Gabel (1984), by providing a platform for creating more adaptive solutions for problems, the examiner can extend the benefits of the present lesson to future sessions involving similar themes.

Case illustration.

Mark S., 12-years-old, was a shy, but affectively labile youngster who had recently entered a special educational treatment center for emotionally disturbed children. The center had a comprehensive school system with a built-in therapy component. It was stated in his social history that Mark was self-absorbed in daydreaming and fantasizing. He was also described as having poor peer relations and as tending to exaggerate stories and constantly blame others for his problems.

During his initial evaluative sessions with a psychiatrist, Mark was reserved and unwilling to disclose much affect. As a way to engage Mark, the psychiatrist introduced the idea of the Draw-A-Story game to gain a better sense of Mark's underlying conflicts and attitudes.

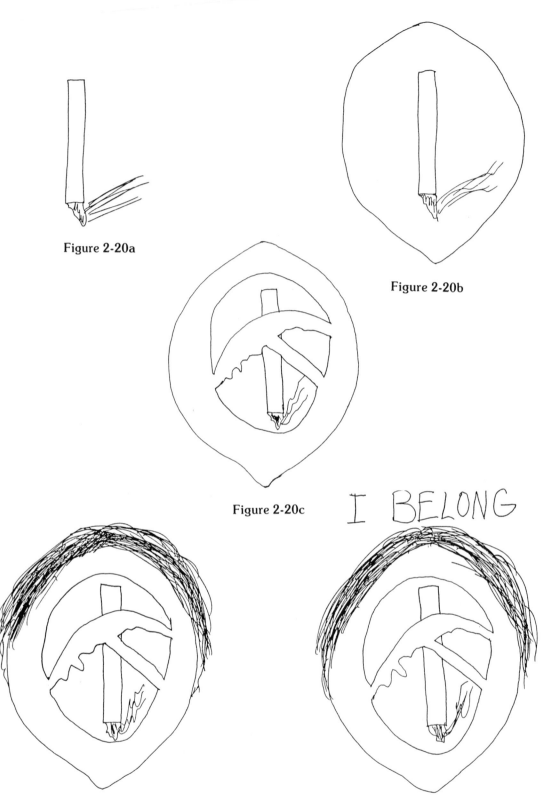

Figure 2-20a

Figure 2-20b

Figure 2-20c

I BELONG

Figure 2-20d

Figure 2-20e

In the first picture, the psychiatrist merely drew a vertical line in the middle of the paper so as to allow maximal direction by Mark. From this line, Mark immediately constructed a cigarette (see Figure 2-20a). Mark then began to tell a story about a boy who had few friends and was yearning for some attachments. "One day," he related, "this boy was approached by other youths in his school to smoke a cigarette." Since it was obvious that Mark was talking about himself through the story, the psychiatrist decided to just draw a circle with the cigarette in the middle in the next picture and allow Mark to continue his story (see Figure 2-20b).

As Mark continued his story he became more relaxed and animated about the struggle that involved him. In fact, in the next picture Mark graphically portrayed his conflict by creating a "no smoking" sign (see Figure 2-20c). He stated to the psychiatrist that this boy was in a "very bad position." He really did not want to smoke but thought he would look foolish and would be rejected if he did not join the other youths in this activity.

The psychiatrist, in following the story, reflected how upset this boy must have been to be experiencing so many contradictory feelings. As he was talking, the psychiatrist added hair to the sign in the picture so that it would be easier for Mark to identify the figure as representing Mark's personal dilemma (see Figure 2-20d).

Finally, Mark added a title to the picture. "I Belong," which was at the crux of his conflict (see Figure 2-20e).

With his creative ability and his newly discovered awareness that he could express himself in this manner, Mark took a significant step towards healthier resolutions of his emotional concerns. He was able to use this type of game to communicate many of the conflicts and inner turmoil he was experiencing. Mark, after this evaluative session, was willing to share his feelings of ambivalence more readily and used this general theme to discuss a variety of emotionally laden topics. From these initial sessions the psychiatrist was able to make substantial recommendations for specific interventions.

CONCLUDING REMARKS

The drawing techniques mentioned in this chapter are only a small sample of the more common ones that have been used clinically over the years to elicit inferences about various aspects of an examinee's personality. Other directives that can be mentioned include, "Draw an unpleasant experience," "Draw a fruit tree," "Draw an animal," "Draw a doodle," "Draw your earliest recollection," and "Draw a dream, mood, feeling, or wish." The drawings that are produced from these directives offer an opportunity to examine the meeting ground of the individual's inner and outer world.

The small amount of time examiners have to spend with people make it imperative to provide as many different types of evaluative experiences as possible. Because there is much evidence to suggest that no single evaluative procedure can provide a comprehensive assessment of cognitive and emotional factors that are affecting a person's performance, clinicians need to be well versed in the special advantages and disadvantages of each procedure they utilize.

Drawings have been incorporated into the standard batteries of most examiners and have stood the test of time, signifying that they do have a special place in providing a richness of information that other tools lack. When drawings are interpreted in the context of other supporting information, knowledgeable examiners can take comfort that they are supplying accurate and thoughtful information to the referral sources. In this manner, appropriate interventions and treatment can then occur.

3

Using Drawings in Individual Psychotherapy

THE VALUE OF DRAWINGS IN PSYCHOTHERAPY

Drawings provide the individual psychotherapist another tool with which to engage the client in self-expression. They give people entering therapy the opportunity to creatively portray their feelings, conflicts, wishes, and so forth. Just as in verbal therapy, the therapist who uses drawings functions primarily in a facilitative role, aiding the individual to explore and discover his/her own capacities for solving conflicts. By allowing a person the freedom of graphic expression, the therapist using drawings offers a challenge for the person to lead the way in the therapeutic process and discover self-direction. The relationship between therapist and client and the latter's own art productions then becomes a catalyst for change.

In providing a warm and supportive environment, therapists who use art can offer to their clients another avenue for release of frustration, aggression, fear, or confusion. By graphically representing some of these feelings, clients bring them out in the open, confront them, and learn to gain control over them. When this has been achieved, individuals in therapy can then begin to feel more in control emotionally, which makes it easier to think for themselves and gain a better sense of identity.

All persons are potentially responsive to the use of drawings in individual psychotherapy. In a manner of speaking, drawings open a door to the unconscious mind, revealing to the therapist issues that are often not verbally expressed. The use of drawings is especially beneficial when working with nonverbal, withdrawn, rageful, and/or resistant clients who may find it easier to express feelings through the art products. Whereas drawings give nonverbal clients an instrument for communication without having to talk, drawings can offer rageful clients, who are often afraid of being overwhelmed by their anger, a safe outlet without fear of becoming destructive. Children are also generally more eager to use art materials, as they are not verbally sophisticated and are not usually capable of insight until later years. Therefore, they can actually reveal and resolve conflicts through the art that otherwise would not be available to them. And, of course, creative individuals who already use art materials for self-expression are usually quite responsive to the use of drawings in therapy.

Therapists who use drawings generally provide goals for the individual entering therapy. By facilitating drawings and discussions surrounding the art products, therapists can help to define and clarify the goals further. However, it is crucial for therapists to listen to their clients' personal interpretations and support their own initiative for change.

BEGINNING PHASES OF PSYCHOTHERAPY

In the early phases of therapy, the behavior and feelings of the individual can most likely be viewed as excessively rigid, as having little focus, as being out of sync, or as being fragmented (Axline, 1969). The therapist's job is to create an environment that allows these individuals to explore their shortcomings in a safe and trusting manner. As therapy progresses, a trust is established which permits the exploration of a broader range of feelings and thoughts. Additionally, a new openness is revealed to the client which can usually be seen in the pictures by less constriction, more honest and accurate thematic portrayals, and greater integration of accepted feelings. Finally, the person experiences a continued enhancement of freedom from disabling limitations of previous strategies of interpersonal functioning and tends to become more psychologically sophisticated and discovers greater potentials within him/herself.

When first entering any kind of therapy, clients may have the expectation that the clinician will have all the answers to their problems and freely offer advice and give magical solutions in the form of a prescription. People in therapy may already have formed beliefs that an alleviation of their problems exists in the teachings of the clinician. By the introduction of art in the early contact, clients quickly learn that they will be responsible for themselves in the relationship and that they can learn to be freer by using the relationship and the drawings as a springboard for greater understanding.

The use of drawings does not influence how often therapists see their clients. However, it may affect the duration of each individual session. Some therapists who use drawings increase the length of sessions to allow enough time for the execution of the drawings. Clients are typically seen once per week unless transference issues are particularly intense or unless they are going through an unusually stressful time. Completion of drawings during each session is encouraged, although it is not necessary.

The use of drawings provides a concrete tool for establishing rapport and for building communication skills during the initial stages of therapy. The use of art materials enhances the expression of feelings, providing a catharticlike atmosphere within the setting. It also seems to increase freer access to unconscious material and reveals conflicts and feelings which may be difficult to express verbally. It is also quite helpful when used for issues pertaining to identification of goals, gauging reality orientation, and measuring problem-solving skills.

THERAPEUTIC CONSIDERATIONS

It is difficult to imagine anyone who cannot benefit from the use of drawings in therapy. However, there are exceptions when care must be taken – for example, patients who are particularly fearful of the revelations from their drawing or patients who have weak ego boundaries. In the latter case, the therapist must provide assurance and only interpret what the patient's fragile ego can handle. The therapist must build on the patient's strengths and provide structure through the drawings. Also, when confronted with resistance by these patients, it may hinder the relationship if the therapist finds him/herself getting into a power struggle over the need to draw. Interpretation of the resistance and suggesting drawings at a later time would be a preferable approach.

It goes without saying, however, that therapists do at times find themselves involved in power struggles with their clients, and sometimes this situation can be punctuated when using drawings. Patients often fear drawings initially, fantasizing that the drawings are like a crystal ball – allowing the therapist to see things that they are not ready to reveal. Sometimes it is helpful to give patients permission not to talk about their drawings initially. Of course, the therapists' expectations are that their patients eventually will share their inner world, but during the beginning of therapy the use of drawings without the demand of talking may promote freer expression and increase spontaneity.

Additionally, it is possible that some clients may be threatened during initial sessions by executing drawings while the therapist observes. If this results in the client being absent from future sessions, the therapist may suggest that he/she do the drawings at home to bring into therapy. It is important to understand, however, that the therapist must continue to request execution of the drawings in the sessions themselves as observation of the process is a crucial aspect of using art as a therapeutic tool.

WHEN THE THERAPIST IS UNAVAILABLE

Art is also an excellent therapeutic tool to use when the therapist is unavailable. For example, if the therapist must miss a session, he/she can suggest specific or free drawings for patients to accomplish at their regularly scheduled time to bring in at a later time. This gives the clients a feeling of continuity even if the therapist is absent. The therapist may even ask clients to do drawings to express how they feel about missing a session or about the therapist's absence. The therapist may also request clients to specify what in their past reminds them of the therapist leaving; or, the therapist may add the directive to draw some of the clients' fantasies of what they believe the therapist will be doing while they are gone, or what fears or anxieties may be produced by the absence. If the therapist is going to be away for several weeks, it may be helpful to assign several drawings, or one that requires more time.

THERAPEUTIC POSTURE WHEN USING DRAWINGS

It is generally best for the therapist to remain a passive, objective observer, especially in the case of a therapist who is not trained in using drawings or other art materials. It is more desirable to obtain as much information, expression of feelings, and self-interpretation from clients about their own drawings before attempting any interpretations. As in all other forms of therapy, it is often better to wait and interpret after a working therapeutic relationship between client and therapist has been established. When using drawings, the therapist must also wait to interpret until the client has completed enough drawings to reveal repetitive themes, consistent patterns, symbols, and so forth. Early interpretations of drawings may cause themes and content of the artwork to become more defensive and stereotypical. In this way, clients may hide behind their art as well. In such cases, some of the advantages that drawings bring to therapy will be lost.

As in regular verbal therapy, clients may bring in their own issues requiring the therapist to be flexible. Often drawings reveal new issues themselves and usually increase the individuals' participation and responsibility in their own therapy. The therapist must be perceptive in recognizing new themes and issues in the art and following through on them. In these cases, it might be helpful to have drawings or themes from the drawings continued from one session to the next as they might increase the person's feelings of continuity in therapy. Also, a more detailed, involved drawing may be therapeutically indicated to enhance the individual's sense of accomplishment and self-control. In general, therapists must follow through on therapeutic goals and themes as they would when working without drawings.

ENCOURAGING SPONTANEITY AND FANTASY

Usually, drawings do not impinge on the individual's spontaneity or verbalizations. In fact, most of the time they do just the opposite. For patients who are resistant or withdrawn, drawings usually give them permission to express themselves freely. As mentioned previously, spontaneity is encouraged with the use of drawings. Possible exceptions to this are artist clients who often use the drawings defensively and compulsive clients who need rulers in attempting to do everything perfectly. In regard to verbalization, drawings usually give clients an object to focus on and enhance their wanting to talk in the sharing of their product. Ernst Kris theorized that in the creative process, the barrier between the Id and Ego becomes "permeable" and therefore unconscious material reaches the pre-conscious more readily (Kris, 1952).

Drawings can also enhance the expression of the person's fantasy life, especially if the therapist promotes a nonjudgmental attitude towards the person's artwork. Typically, these drawings help therapists and patients see how their fantasy lives impact on daily functioning, decision making, goals, and so forth. However, with psychotic or prepsychotic individuals, as well as persons who tend to escape into their fantasy life, drawings may be too threatening and/or reinforcing and, therefore, detrimental and contraindicated. It is relevant to mention that in all cases of drawings used to express fantasy life, a separate drawing should be done to represent reality for comparison (see case illustration at the end of this chapter for an example of this cautionary note).

ENCOURAGING GROWTH

An important aspect of the process of psychotherapy is intrapersonal and interpersonal growth, and in this regard drawings add to the individual's experiences, which alter the person's perspective and focus. This change is constantly evolving and assuming varying degrees of importance within the personality of the individual, which is continually assimilating and accommodating new insights into different attitudes, thoughts, and feelings. Drawings add considerably to this process as they can become concrete markers in this chain of events leading to health.

A quote by Virginia Axline (1969) might further define this concept of health:

> When the individual develops sufficient self-confidence to bring his self-concept out of the shadow land and into the sun and consciously and purposefully to direct his behavior by evaluation, selectivity, and application to achieve his ultimate goal in life, i.e., complete self-realization, then he seems to be well organized. (p. 13)

PROVIDING A PLATFORM FOR THERAPEUTIC CHANGE

A fundamental goal in therapeutic change is to provide a nonthreatening environment which is conducive to helping a person function more fully. Before working towards that goal, people in therapy must initially become cognizant of the roles they perform or "public masks" they wear during their daily activities. To thwart inner turmoil or anxiety, most people have to develop pretenses or façades and in this process of deception these people become estranged from themselves (Rogers, 1961). One technique that might be helpful to the clinician who introduces drawings into the relationship is to employ the directive, "Draw your mask and what is behind it." At first, clients may balk at such a direct onslaught on their public image, but motivated people will probably appreciate the opportunity to explore their daily "mask(s)" in an uncritical atmosphere. (See example in Chapter 5.)

The use of drawings is designed to allow the person in therapy to become "unstuck" and to "do something." It is a technique implemented to force action and provide a source of satisfaction and accomplishment. The graphic expression of the drawing thus becomes the instrument for change. The therapist does not have preconceived roles but allows the freedom of the continuing relationship to develop. Drawings provide the focal point for this change to occur and offer an ongoing record of the experience. The minimal direction that a therapist employs in a drawing directive should give the necessary freedom to explore parts of the person's life that is not being accurately perceived or realized. The outcome of this strategy allows the person to lower defenses and become open to other possibilities that exist and are attainable.

By opening up to new experiences, which various drawing directives provide, individuals in therapy begin to see more concrete forms of reality without the distortions that verbal defenses offer. It is within this process that clients begin slowly to change and become more flexible in thoughts and ideas. This, in turn, provides further knowledge which allows a greater tolerance of ambiguity. In this manner, the drawings offer persons in therapy an opportunity to experience themselves in newer and fresher ways.

According to Rogers (1961), to engage in therapy is a "process of becoming," and the person in therapy soon realizes that the process is ongoing. Rather than being in a static relationship, clients begin to grasp the fluidity of change as their perceptions and beliefs are constantly in transition and revision. Drawings document this ongoing procedure and add the opportunity for many timely interpretations and discussions.

INTERPRETATION AND RELATIONSHIP BUILDING

Drawings can become excellent tools for interpretation because they are permanent and cannot be as easily denied. Because they are graphic, clients can clearly "see" the therapist's method of interpretation. In order to gain insight through artwork, it is important to use the artwork metaphorically and to use the clients' symbols in dialogue with them. In some cases, interpretation by the therapist is not as essential since the artwork itself enhances the ability to develop personal insight through the images. It is also sometimes necessary for the therapist to retrieve old drawings for interpretation, or to show their clients how they have changed. This is why it is important to date and keep all the drawings. Another point to keep in mind is that when an interpretation of a drawing is made, it may be helpful to ask the client if he/she would like to either change the drawing itself or do another drawing to indicate the possibility presented and/or the potential for change.

The establishment of a therapeutic relationship is accomplished through the therapist's nonjudgmental, supportive, empathic responses to the clients' sharing of their drawings. Hanging artwork, for example, can underline the person's significance; or placing emphasis on keeping the artwork in a safe, private folder stresses the idea of confidentiality in the relationship and aids in this process. Dual drawings – that is, the therapist drawing along with the individual – can sometimes be helpful in this phase, especially if the client is withdrawn or resistant (and if the therapist minimizes his/her own contributions). Supporting any accomplishments by the client, no matter how insignificant, is also salient to the establishment of the relationship, and this process can be emphasized by having the person draw how he/she "feels" about personal success. (See Figure 3-1.)

Anne M., age 12, had just been transferred to a male therapist after spending the past eight months with a woman therapist. Anne approached the initial therapeutic sessions with a very guarded, defensive stance and would not talk. Because of her nervousness the therapist offered her the opportunity to draw with him, which she readily accepted. This approach provided Anne with a nonthreatening way to interact with her new therapist and gave her an example of how therapy can be effective using different approaches. The drawing in Figure 3-1 is a result of this working together. Anne, who was very anxious and controlling, at first drew only the ominous-looking clouds at the top of the paper to indicate her uncertainty of the situation. Before the therapist added anything to the drawing, Anne used the remaining colored markers to add a smiling sun and the words "Jerry's Jeep." With a feeling of accomplishment (and relief that she could take such risks to gain some control) she then "allowed" the therapist to add to the drawing, but only with the remaining space. The therapist added the road and picture of a jeep to "join" with this resistant child.

RESOLVING CONFLICTS

It is also during the initial process of therapy that the therapist explores which of those defenses identified during the evaluative period may be helpful to their clients and which ones seem to be blocking their growth. If the clients are inhibited, and avoid and deny any problems, it may be evident from their drawings, which appear without change in their manner of execution or content. Strengths and weaknesses of these guarded individuals may be identified by directing them to draw symbols that represent these characteristics. The drawings can then serve as a vehicle for unresolved past feelings which generalize to the present in the form of concrete representations.

An example of how a resolution of a particular conflict may be supported is by asking clients to either draw fantasies of their anger being acted out, or construct symbols for their anger. Drawings provide a safe place to express this anger and are not harmful to anyone when done privately in an

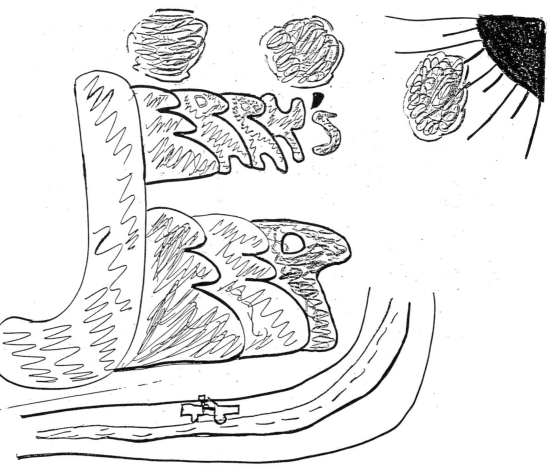

Figure 3-1

individual session. Often, later in the stage of relationship building, the therapist will see an increase of emotions expressed in the drawings. Displays of cathartic release and some regression may occur. Individuals at this time may lose control in their drawing, scribbling furiously. Acceptance by the therapist in these cases is shown by encouraging clients to make something out of their scribbles, thus enhancing the sublimation process, which has as its goal the mature expression of overwhelming feelings. Figure 3-2 illustrates this process.

Hank W., age 13, was being seen in therapy due to his relentless anger, which was usually directed towards his father. In one animated session in which drawing was used as a primary medium because of Hank's difficulty in verbally expressing his feelings, he was able to construct the drawing in Figure 3-2 and naturally entitled it, "Just Me and My Dad." At first he only drew the large space rocket in the middle as a symbol of the power he perceived his father as possessing. Soon he began to draw attacking planes which set off a frantic pace of additional planes and support to defeat this large vehicle. Only minimal self-control and the end of the session stopped this picture from becoming an elaborate scribble.

USING ALTERNATIVE ART MEDIA

Total catharsis and regression in art are often dependent on the kind of art media being employed. These processes (i.e., catharsis and regression) do not occur as often when drawing is used as the sole basis for expression. They are more likely to happen with fingerpaint or clay. Unless trained specifically in art therapy, rarely would the mental health professional use these types of materials for such purposes.

The drawing medium itself introduces another element in the individual therapeutic relationship. Namely the person is given materials that enhance his/her independent functioning within the relationship. Judith Rubin, an eminent art therapist, believes that when art materials are used it is more difficult for the therapist to remain neutral in the transference relationship because of the effect of giving the person the materials. In this way, she hypothesizes, the therapist becomes "feeder" . . . "seducer" . . . , and has "expectations" for the patient (Rubin, 1978, p. 271).

EXPRESSIONS OF TRANSFERENCE

The idea of transference is important for the mental health professional to consider when involved in art. Often a theme within the art product or the color being used can represent previous experiences to the individual in

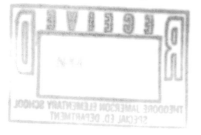

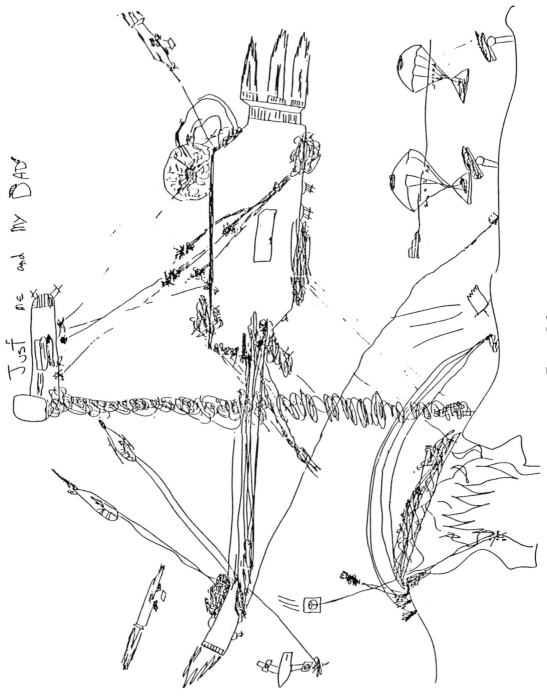

Figure 3-2

treatment. This is not dissimilar to a person projecting thoughts or feelings onto other people (Rubin, 1978). Transference to the therapist is sometimes evident in the drawings themselves or sometimes expressed in the aggressive use of the art materials. Patients may actually draw the therapist or draw themselves with some personal aspect changed to resemble the therapist – for example, a symbolic representation of ambivalence, anger at authority figures, or resistance. The following two drawings illustrate this phase of the therapeutic process. Both drawings were begun without specific direction.

This symbolic rendering of the solar system (see Figure 3-3), completed by a 15-year-old male inpatient who had been admitted because of threatening to rape his mother, seemed to be an indicator of the transference relationship between him and his female therapist (the art therapist co-author). The larger circular drawing represented himself, the smaller one the therapist (which was his own interpretation). It is interesting to note that the smaller solar system is partially off the paper. This appeared to represent his difficulty responding to limits, as it was hard for him to remain on the paper. He indicated that he felt particularly happy about this drawing and his feelings about therapy since it was very difficult for him to establish mature relationships and experience a sense of trust, especially with maternal figures.

This drawing (Figure 3-4), completed by the same Hank W. as in Figure 3-2, was done further along in the therapeutic process. Although his intense anger remained, it was beginning to be displaced in other arenas outside the household. In this example, appropriately entitled "Watch Out Therapists, Here I Come," his anger was beginning to be more directed at the therapist and other persons in perceived positions of authority. The added scribbling possibly indicated that this process was anxiety-provoking to him, as he was not sure of the consequences of unleashing his anger on other adults besides his father. This was illustrated by the therapist's addition (this was also a dual drawing) of an enclosed dome with a man meditating inside (lower right corner). This infuriated and frustrated Hank as he was much more used to direct attacks by his father. The therapist (the psychologist co-author) also added a title at the bottom of the drawing, "The Anger That Never Ends," which stimulated many discussions around this central feeling in future sessions.

This brings up an important point to consider when introducing drawings into the therapeutic relationship, that is, whether to actively engage in drawings with the client. When therapists draw along with their clients, the clients may feel that their therapists are not giving them the undivided

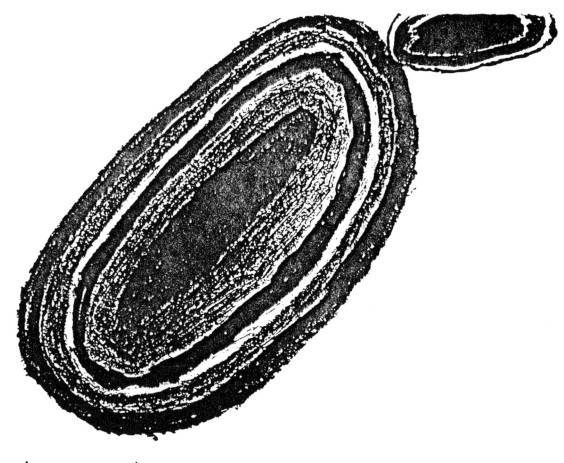

HAPPY SOLOR SysTem

Figure 3-3

attention they desire. As previously shown, dual drawings are helpful if the clients are especially resistant, withdrawn, or having difficulty establishing a therapeutic relationship and nothing else seems to work. When therapists participate in dual drawings, they are essentially lending their own ego strength. If dual drawings are indicated, therapists must be careful about what they contribute. If the drawing is realistic, the therapist must make objects that enhance and support the client's ideas, such as establishing groundlines, trying not to determine what course the drawing will take, and encouraging the client's own ideas. If the drawing is abstract, the therapist

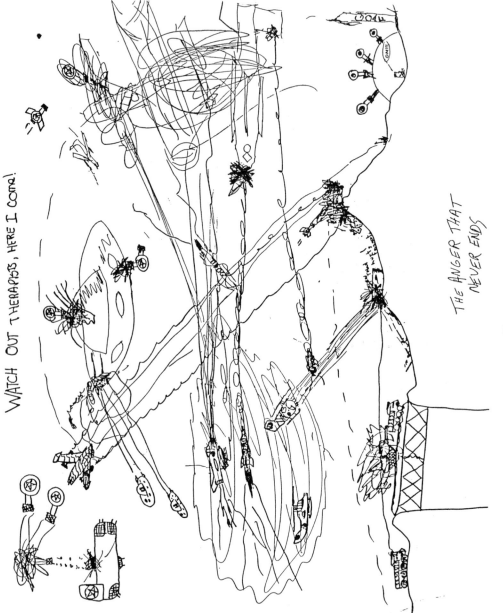

WATCH OUT THERAPISTS, HERE I come!

THE ANGER THAT NEVER ENDS

Figure 3-4

would have the same considerations but would also have to be more careful, as abstraction tends to increase freer expression and has the potential of reducing the therapist's objectivity.

WORKING-THROUGH PROCESS

An important stage within psychotherapy is the concept of the working-through process. This process can be described as the resolution of unconscious conflicts and repressed feelings which gives clients insight into their maladaptive behaviors and leads to more adaptive and satisfying experiences. Successfully working through a problem can provide the person in treatment with experiential evidence that contact with others can be mutually satisfying and therefore worth developing. "Before, during, and after" drawings of the therapeutic experience may help clients actually view their working-through process in a symbolic and valid manner. The execution of these drawings often decreases a defensive posture which allows the freer expression of unconscious and/or repressed conflicts.

Doug H., age 13, was admitted into a residential treatment center after being hospitalized for one month due to out-of-control behavior including fire-setting. Since he already had considerable therapy while in the hospital, his primary therapist, a social worker, asked him what he had gained from the experience. Because he was distractible and highly anxious in the new setting, he was unable to offer much insight into these probing questions. Discovering that Doug enjoyed drawing, the therapist suggested that he attempt a "before, during, and after" sequence of drawings related to the hospitalization. Doug immediately responded to this directive by quickly drawing (probably due to his nervousness and fear of being judged) a set of four pictures which captured his insight about what went on and what he was not able to verbalize.

The first panel (see Figure 3-5a) was a drawing of his family, with him in complete control. By his perception, his parents were not able to handle his ferocity and he viewed his younger brother as insignificant. The next two drawings (see Figures 3-5b,c) illustrate the consequences of his anger, that is, being hospitalized. Once in the hospital he seemed to indicate that he was still acting wild (pillow fight) but this activity was controlled (the bars over the window). Ironically he portrayed his parents as celebrating his absence and their ultimate authority. In the final drawing (see Figure 3-5d), Doug expressed a changed dynamic in the family following his treatment.

Figure 3-5a

This drawing suggested that now the father was the one expressing his anger (figure on left with teeth), with the mother and more significant little brother also agitating him. For his part, Doug had become overly controlled and, although still extremely angry, would not allow himself to verbally express his thoughts, that is, "screw off." With this information, both Doug and the therapist were able to discuss some of these new insights.

Another example of the working-through process is a drawing completed by a 12-year-old boy, Aaron P., who had been admitted into a children's unit of a general hospital for school refusal and not eating. He came reluctantly to an initial therapy session with his primary therapist, a child psychiatrist, not wanting to do anything because he was "bored". When the psychiatrist asked Aaron to draw "what being "bored" would look like, he was surprised to find himself drawing a cloud that was raining tears (see Figure 3-6). He then became tearful and revealed that his mother, who promised she would visit him, had called to cancel. The therapist was able to interpret his feelings of sadness and rejection and how he usually defended himself from these feelings. From there she suggested how he might find himself acting out his anger by his passive-aggressive stance of being "bored" and not doing anything. Without the directive to draw the experience of boredom that Aaron was admitting, this insight would not have been as easily integrated for this particular youth. He actually used the drawing to work

78

Figure 3-5b

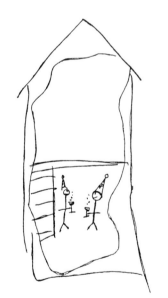

Figure 3-5c

Figure 3-5d

through his underlying feelings of sadness and rejection. When introduced at key moments, the directive to draw a feeling can be a vital learning process.

ENDING THERAPY

In the termination phase of therapy, individuals are often asked to review all their artwork and draw how they see themselves changed by therapy. A "before and after" drawing may also help people assess their changes as well (see Figure 3-7). This directive provides concrete markers for clients to observe their progress.

Figure 3-6

The illustration in Figure 3-7, drawn by a 13-year-old male inpatient with a diagnosis of elective mutism, was completed during his final therapeutic sessions in the hospital. The directive to construct a "before and after" drawing revealed some of the insights gained in the therapeutic experience. For example, when he chose not to talk he realized he was protecting himself and attempting to control his environment. However, his defensive manner did not make him feel happy or satisfied, as shown by the facial expression on the left side of the drawing. He had also realized that when he talked to others he felt less protected, but was happier. He had learned ways of feeling more in control by talking to people whom he felt he could trust. Needless to say, using art with this boy who would not talk was a very successful method of helping him learn to communicate without having to talk directly.

Before ending an individual therapeutic relationship, it is also helpful to ask clients to draw how they see themselves in the future, what future goals they may have, and so on, to support their independence from therapy and from the therapist. It is common to observe a client's ambivalence surrounding leaving portrayed in his/her final drawings, and much richness can be gained in discussions about the drawings during these final sessions.

Figure 3-7

USING DRAWINGS IN BRIEF PSYCHOTHERAPY
AND CRISIS INTERVENTION

The therapist using drawings in individual treatment must be well versed in both longer-term, in-depth modalities, as well as brief, more focused techniques to confront crisis situations and acute emotional upheaval. Examples of short-term therapeutic issues include such situational problems as a suicide attempt leading to hospitalization, an acute drug reaction, medical illness, loss of a job leading to personal dissatisfaction and family disharmony, relocation, death of a significant other, and separation and divorce. These can all become problems when the person in crisis cannot immediately resolve his/her conflicts and his/her psychosocial resources become strained.

Because the therapeutic intervention is time-limited and focused on a single issue, there are differences in how drawings are utilized. For example, the drawing directives used usually do not have to address such longer-term issues as transference. It is more helpful if the drawings simply help people identify and clarify their problem areas or crises that led them into therapy. Another use of drawings in brief therapy may be to identify any past problems, memories, anniversary dates, and so on, which may relate to recent problems. Asking clients to draw their strengths, social supports, and current and past manner of coping can be quite helpful when considering short-term strategies.

For example, an 11-year-old boy, Mike L., was requested to draw his perceived strengths as part of a more comprehensive evaluation during his brief treatment as an inpatient (see Figure 3-8). Because of his poor self-esteem and unwillingness to present himself as having many strengths, the evaluator had to support and clarify many of his stronger characteristics before he proceeded to draw anything. In fact, the first picture Mike drew (lower left of Figure 3-8) was of his mother, with whom he had what appeared to be a pathologically dependent relationship. By asking Mike to selectively attend to his strengths, the therapist allowed him the opportunity to concretely see that he had more assets than he previously had believed. This directive provided Mike and his therapist with specific goals to work towards in helping him gain some semblance of independent functioning.

Drawings give individuals in shorter-term treatment another language with which to "cognitively" work out their problems, enhancing their ability to reintegrate independently. Drawings also enhance the expression of feelings which helps people towards problem resolution. In turn, this also helps therapists evaluate how realistically their clients are coming to terms with their problems and whether or not longer-term treatment is warranted. Also, in brief psychotherapy, goals can be expressed and determined symbolically in drawings. It can be quite helpful to ask the client to execute a "past, present, future" drawing to enhance awareness of personal responsibility and continuity. Another directive can be to request the drawing of a past similar problem that relates to the current crisis. Basically these direc-

Figure 3-8

tives follow a crisis information model (Caplan, 1964; Lindemann, 1944). That is, the focus of the intervention is oriented towards problem solving rather than curing emotional illness. Overall, drawings used in brief psychotherapy are most helpful when used for supporting clarification and coping rather than exploring deeper issues.

Steve M. was a 28-year-old white male who had a history of prior hospitalizations due to recurring depressive episodes. During a brief stay as an inpatient, he was directed by his primary therapist to construct a drawing of his "past, present, future" (see Figure 3-9). From this picture (which he

Figure 3-9

drew from right to left), he was able to pictorially depict and later express his feelings regarding his periods of depression and was able to portray some optimism concerning his view of the future. On the right of the picture is an ominous storm approaching. The actual storm, or what he was presently experiencing, was portrayed by lightning striking. His feelings of helplessness and vulnerability were expressed by his running (in actuality, these were times when he would become self-destructive and would be hospitalized).

CASE ILLUSTRATION

The following case example explores more of the issues raised in this chapter and guides the reader through the various phases of a therapeutic relationship, offering key drawing directives which can be used at crucial times to increase the progress being made in treatment. Interpretations are limited since it is often helpful to the reader to explore his/her own theoretical orientation when viewing fresh drawings.

The case presented here is of a 17-year-old adolescent male, David B., who was in an inpatient state psychiatric hospital. He was diagnosed by the psychiatrist on the adolescent unit as having a Conduct Disorder, classified as undersocialized and aggressive according to the third version of the APA Diagnostic and Statistical Manual of Mental Disorders (DSM-III), and was admitted to the hospital due to aggressive tendencies which verged on paranoia. An arsenal of stolen weapons was discovered in his bedroom, supposedly to be used for his own protection. He had been formally charged by the police with breaking and entering and auto theft, and he purportedly displayed suicidal ideation following his arrest. He was court-ordered to the adolescent unit of the hospital for evaluation and treatment.

David had already been hospitalized for approximately one year prior to entering into a therapeutic relationship where drawings were used as a primary focus in treatment. He had been drawing independently quite a bit on the adolescent unit of the hospital and he had been attending open art therapy groups consistently on his own. This particular approach to individual treatment took approximately eight months. During the beginning phase of therapy, David appeared anxious, executing his drawings quickly, and tended to be highly self-critical. He rarely was able to provide direct eye contact, and he also had difficulty articulating his thoughts. Apparently he had had a severe speech problem as a child, which still manifested itself during adolescence.

In drawing an initial self-portrait (a directive given to project a personal image of the self), David portrayed a muscular figure that had been cut and sutured (see Figure 3-10). Next to this picture of himself was a bloody sword stuck in the ground. This large muscular figure drawn to represent himself was somewhat grandiose and unrealistic since David himself was small in stature. In this case he was possibly compensating for a personal sense of inadequacy. The blood, cuts, and sword seemed to be representative of the intensity of his underlying anger. He even described himself as having "gory and violent fantasies."

At the time, the therapist concluded that David had intense self-destructive fantasies, as he had drawn himself alone with the sword, but the sword was not in his hand, which might have indicated denial of his impulses. Also, his strong emphasis on the belt and zipper of his pants seemed to suggest possible anxiety related to issues concerning sexuality. His somewhat compulsive attention to detail was also evident in this initial drawing, possibly indicating his strong need for controls over his underlying anger, anxiety, and confusion.

Next, David's paranoid fantasies were projected onto his scribble drawing which was completed during his individual art evaluation when he first

Figure 3-10

entered the hospital (see Figure 3-11). He outlined two large eyes and entitled it the "Beholder."

Through these evaluative drawings and David's spontaneous verbalizations, the therapist was able to conclude early in therapy that David was additionally conflicted regarding themes of good and evil and had an intense need to defend, hide, and/or escape into fantasy. (Later examples will illustrate these points.) Through contact with David's and his parents' family therapist, it was noted that David's parents were also struggling and they would often pull David into the center of these conflicts. He seemed to view his parents in a kind of "borderline split" of good and bad. He saw his mother as the good person, although the father played a dominant role in the family. His mother, it was later discovered, tended to align herself with David in a seductive manner and was openly critical of the father, often using David to get back at him. Also, it seemed that David perceived his mother as fantasy-oriented like himself and his father as logical and controlling. In this way, David also reinforced the mother-son alliance. His identification with the mother was obvious in the rich fantasy that was expressed through his drawings. His need for controls was also quite apparent in his artwork, as demonstrated by his attention to detail and his desire for perfection, as well as his consistent choice of pencil as his preferred medium for expression.

Following a consultation with the family therapist, the art therapist agreed that David's part in his parents' conflicts would be explored in family therapy. The individual therapist then decided to focus on using David's drawings as a method for expressing his individual needs, underlying anger, and confusion. David's drawings also were used to: 1) explore his maladaptive ways of coping with his anger; 2) test out reality in a supportive atmosphere; 3) strengthen his self-esteem by supporting his art skills; and 4) support his identity formation by delineating his likes and dislikes, by viewing his confusions surrounding relationships, and so forth. (Due to the quantity of work executed during the course of therapy, this presentation will primarily focus on David's use of fantasy in relation to his anger, issues of transference, and the termination phase of his therapy.)

Because of David's tendency to escape into his fantasy life, the therapist introduced the idea of constructing a series of drawings to represent his "worst fantasy," "best reality," and "best fantasy." By providing these directives, the therapist believed that David would be able to develop insight into this tendency and learn more adaptive ways of coping with reality. David chose to work on his "best fantasy" first (see Figure 3-12).

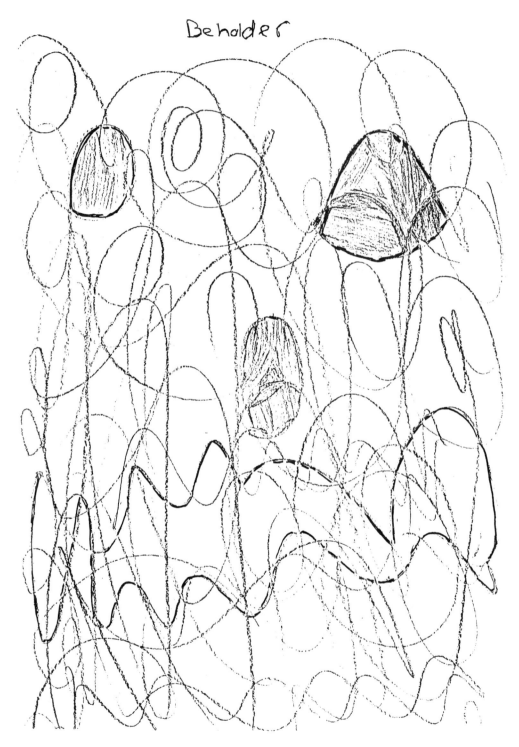

Figure 3-11

Figure 3-12

This drawing was of the "future" where everyone lived underground; again, it represented his need to withdraw. According to David, the space station on top of the mountains protected the people underground from the enemy who lived on the planet (upper right hand corner). The therapist may be able to obtain more information by asking the patient what was behind the mountains. David revealed that this was the source of the river. Rivers were a repetitive theme in David's drawings. Based on many discussions about the use of this symbol, the therapist was able to conclude that they represented "a way out" of the picture, again indicative of David's need to escape unpleasant circumstances.

The therapist then directed David to draw his "best reality" (see Figure 3-13). In this drawing, David constructed a city street with business establishments whose names included issues that were significant within the process of David's identity formation, that is, references to art, values, and home. The drawing is very similar in quality to the previous ones in its detail, and in its inclusion of another escape route (an alley). The building

Figure 3-13

90

on the left was meant to be the home of a wealthy, eccentric businessman. Overall, it seemed that David tended to fantasize even in his depiction of reality. There were electronic eyes above the electric garage door for viewing visitors and all the windows were shaded. He also verbally indicated that if visitors did not have the right password the door would "cut them in half" as they entered. All of the above reemphasized David's experiencing a high degree of suspiciousness and as possessing aggressive tendencies.

David then chose to draw his "worst reality" (see Figure 3-14). His attention to detail is again exhibited by such qualities as including cigarette butts on the ground in front of the bench. The line quality seemed to indicate that he was more anxious about the execution of this particular drawing than previous ones. There are clouds blocking the sun, possibly symbolizing his more conscious acts of aggression. Also, he drew himself seated on the bench. During the session, David had been talking about running away. When he drew himself seated on the bench, the therapist

Figure 3-14

91

concluded that actually David was ambivalent about leaving the hospital (which was true).

Finally, the therapist had David draw his "worst fantasy" (see Figure 3-15). This drawing was very difficult for David to execute. He appeared unusually tense and anxious. What is included in the drawing is a sacrificial altar. There are two victims of the sacrifice. The one on the left is the body of the victim who had his heart torn out on the altar. On the altar there is a heart and the gruesome tools used in the procedure. The body on the left is the person who attempted to save the one being sacrificed. David then

Figure 3-15

dipped the entire piece of paper in a wash of red paint to represent the enormous amount of blood everywhere.

He then, with great difficulty, revealed that this drawing represented a recurring dream that he had been experiencing. He had always been afraid that the sacrificed person in the dream was himself and that anyone who tried to help him was in grave danger. This probably represented his own feelings of worthlessness which were apparent during his treatment. This drawing was a tremendous step in David's therapy. First, he revealed his worst fears. Second, it possibly signified the beginning of a therapeutic relationship, as someone was there to help him; but also his ultimate fear was disclosed in that he believed that help was not a real possibility since whoever attempted to help him would be destroyed.

The therapist then had David begin a drawing in which he integrated all four of the above fantasies (see Figure 3-16). The therapist's goal with this kind of drawing was to help David see that he did not necessarily have to "split" and withdraw into his fantasies. The therapist supported David's imagination as a strength but also suggested that it could be used in a more adaptive way.

This drawing was continued throughout David's therapy. It tended to reflect his progress in therapy. He began by drawing the mountains and river of his best fantasy. These probably gave him a sense of security. He then added the hospital in the upper left hand area of the drawing. On top of the mountain he drew the space station. He then indicated that he had made the space station larger to represent the importance of his fantasy life. Next he drew two abductors from his "worst fantasy," chasing the victim towards a hole in the ground on the right. The therapist questioned why he had included a hole in the ground as there was not a hole in any of his previous drawings. He indicated that the hole gave the victim a place to hide. (To include the sacrificial altar would probably have made David too anxious.) The city on the lower left was the city of his "best reality."

The rich eccentric in this story had moved out of the city into the castle below the space station. The eccentric's helicopter had "razor sharp" runners so that no one could possibly climb aboard. Again, David got carried away with his type of paranoid, aggressive fantasies. The therapist directed David to connect all of the realities in such a way as to stress the importance of integrating these pictures. He drew a road and then a bridge over the river.

In the several sessions it took to execute the above drawing, David had been complaining about "boredom" on the adolescent unit and anger at the staff and the other clinicians. The therapist directed David to make a draw-

Escape
from
the Fantasy

Figure 3-16

ing of himself as "bored" in an attempt to gain fuller insight into this feeling (see Figure 3-17). At first he drew himself seated, smoking cigarettes, and lying on his bed. He next drew himself (on the right) seated and smoking cigarettes, and added a large cloud hovering over his head. He then spontaneously began drawing symbols for thoughts he had when "bored." He was amazed at how angry these symbols appeared to him. The insight that "boredom" possibly masked his anger quickly followed. He then turned the cloud into an angry dragon breathing fire. (It is also significant to note that he included the hills of his fantasy life in the lower left foot of the dragon to symbolize his need to withdraw from such overwhelming feelings.)

It was during this time in therapy that David symbolically and angrily destroyed the hospital in his large drawing (see Figure 3-16). It might be

Figure 3-17

mentioned that it was important for him to save a few people (including the therapist) prior to the bombing. He also gave the hospital a laser to fight back, but he ultimately won. While constructing this drawing, he shared his anger, which he perceived as resulting from his freedom being taken away as an inpatient. In addition, he expressed his anger and frustration at his parents and discussed his anxiety concerning his inability to trust others. This lack of trust appeared to have stemmed from traumatic childhood experiences.

The therapist then had David execute a drawing that would directly symbolize his anger (see Figure 3-18). By this time in his treatment, David appreciated the opportunity to use the art media in a mature way to help him with his problems and was willing to attempt any drawing that his therapist requested. The opportunity to draw his feelings offered David a safe outlet to display his intense rage. In this sketch, David's feelings of anger appeared as a big, floating, flaming ball. He also drew himself coming out of the hole (in the ground behind him) to confront his anger.

Figure 3-18

Following this drawing directive, the therapist asked David to symbolically represent control over his anger so as to reduce his feelings of being overwhelmed by his impulses. This directive, in a metaphorical way, attempted to get David to think that he could have control over them (see Figure 3-19). The anger expressed in this picture is portrayed as a chained monster housed in a cage on top of a mountain. It is controlled by David (on the right) by the antenna on his head. He is at a safe distance and holds a gun. It is interesting that David referred to the monster affectionately, expressing its need to be protected from others as well as others being protected from it. This statement probably represented his own fears and needs for structure and an environment free from stressors.

Figure 3-19

David also noted that "the anger is all that keeps the monster alive." This statement might have represented David's belief that if he were not able to be angry he might have become so depressed he would have attempted suicide. David also realized at the time that his drawings had become less "gory and violent."

Following the preceding drawings of his anger, David began to bring in objects he had found outside of the hospital which, for him, portrayed reality but could also contain fantasies. For example, he brought in a weathered piece of wood. He pointed out one area of the wood and asked the therapist to imagine it as the landscape of another planet. It seemed that David was beginning to integrate fantasy and reality. The therapist then suggested that he do landscape drawings onto which he could superimpose his fantasies (see Figure 3-20).

Again, we see in this drawing David's cave, a repeated symbol for his

Figure 3-20

withdrawal. However, we can now observe him sitting at the entrance, visible and not totally withdrawn. It is significant that other than the hole in the rock to depict the cave, David was very careful to reproduce exactly what he observed. Emphasis on the crack in the rock again shows his attention to detail. However, for the first time David used chalk instead of a pencil to construct this drawing. He did not seem overly concerned about its tendency to smear, possibly indicating a reduced need for control. The woods are "dense for hiding" and the "barbarian is tending his fire to ward off animals and guard his cave."

Although this drawing still tended to have a paranoid flavor, it seemed less severe and more appropriate to the setting. The fire was also smaller, possibly reflecting David's previous expression of his anger having been somewhat reduced. Following this drawing, David performed an entire series of realistic drawings of the mountains. Although these landscapes still included elements of his previous drawings (e.g., mountains and emptiness), they were considerably less fantasy-oriented and contained less symbolic expressions of anger (see Figure 3-21). This drawing was entitled, "A Longing for Freedom." David shared with the therapist that he had often looked at the mountains outside his hospital room for over a year.

It was at this time that transference issues in David's therapy seemed to have reached their height. In the next picture, he drew himself being sucked into a "whirlpool" (see Figure 3-22). The therapist asked him to attach another drawing to this one that could represent some alternative to being sucked into the whirlpool in order to enhance his coping skills. He drew "a savior" on the shore pulling him out. In Figure 3-23, David drew himself as falling through the clouds towards the volcano and dragon below (see Figure 3-23).

David revealed that the volcano and dragon symbolized his anger. The drawing was entitled "Limbo," which represented his confusion about whether or not there was a possibility for him to be discharged from the hospital. He then added a rope with a "friendly demon" attached who would catch him. The demon had sharp claws, probably indicative of David's ambivalent feelings towards therapy.

Next, David was able to gain some insight regarding his fears through a drawing (see Figure 3-24). In this picture, a "holy man" (possibly representing the therapist) is exorcizing a ghost that seemed to represent fear. Once again the volcano, a recurring symbol for David's anger, was in the background. There was a paranoid quality about the drawing in terms of the religious ideation in its content. Symbolically, through the support of these characters, David was able to confront his fear and title his drawing, "Fear of Nothing," which was more specifically subtitled, "Nothing to Fear but Fear Itself." This drawing seemed to indicate some underlying ego strength and a new found ability to confront his fear.

As David's discharge date from the hospital was approaching, he became overwhelmed by feelings of helplessness, anxiety, and ambivalence. To share these experiences he was again requested to draw a self-portrait since he continued to have difficulty verbalizing troubled thoughts and feelings. He represented these feelings in a portrait of himself seemingly split in half (see Figure 3-25). The right side of the page represented the residential treatment center he was going to be attending in the future. He described this as "unknown and scary." The left side represented the hospital, which he described as "friends, knowing things, and comfortable." Overall the picture was indicative of how anxious and overwhelmed he must have been feeling. There were many unidentifiable shapes and it was highly disorganized.

Figure 3-21

Figure 3-22

The therapist supported David in confronting these fears by asking him to draw a picture of the "unknown" (see Figure 3-26). In this exercise, David drew himself (back facing the viewer) looking through a "doorway to?" There was a strong shadow to indicate a powerful light outside the door, which David described as "blinding." He expressed his need to "have a little time for my eyes to adjust." This was probably David's way of saying he needed some time to adjust to the fact he was going to be discharged. Often, when the back of a figure faces the viewer there is some denial; therefore, the therapist directed David to draw the other side of the door (i.e., a frontal view of himself), which can be seen in Figure 3-27.

Although he was able to draw the figure, the line quality in the drawing

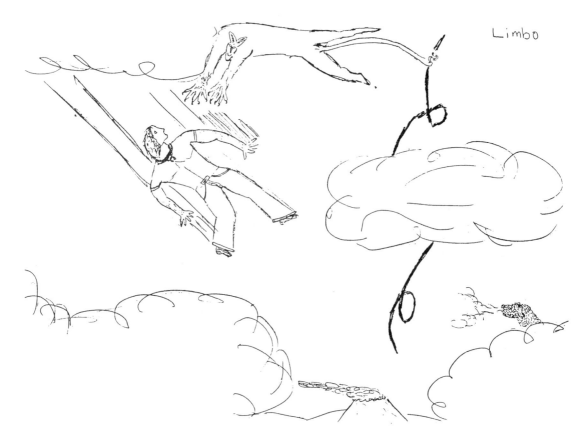

Figure 3-23

appeared to reflect his heightened nervousness as well as his increased need for control as observed by his attention to detail. It seemed that David could not imagine any real objects on the other side of the door. The therapist and he then discussed what it would probably be like to leave, and the therapist arranged to have David visit the treatment center to reduce his anxiety.

Figure 3-24

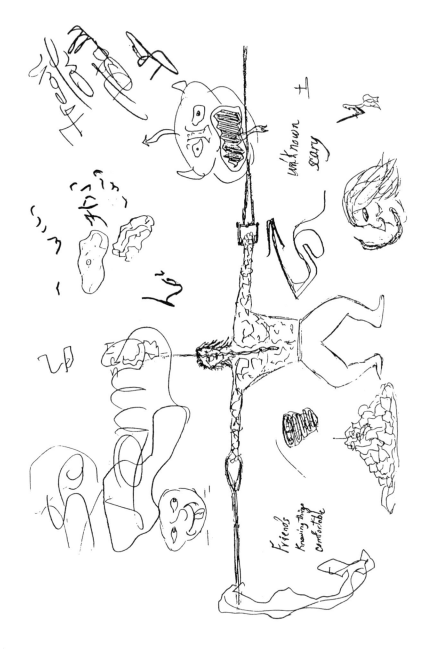

Figure 3-25

Finally, David spontaneously completed his large drawing prior to leaving therapy (refer back to Figure 3-16). First he added a range of mountains behind the hospital to represent the "promised land" (the future). He and two friends (small penciled figures between the explosion and space station) were pictured as crawling towards this "promised land." He then destroyed the space station and castle with flames. He also closed up the

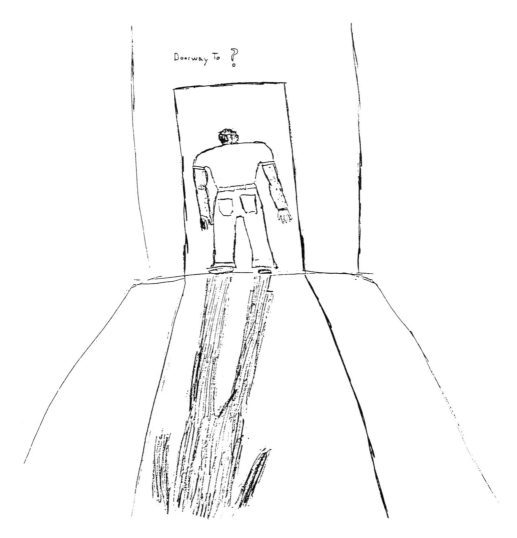

Figure 3-26

hole in the ground and protected his victim by drawing the large black barricade. He then added another piece in the road (middle) to connect the roads on the reality side of the drawing. He also burned out the bridge on the fantasy side. Finally, he entitled the drawing, "Escape from Fantasy." Therefore, David symbolically stated his desire to leave behind his tendency to withdraw into fantasies as a coping mechanism and to continue on to his "promised land."

In summary, through his drawings David was able to gain insight into why he used his fantasy life to reduce tension. He was able to gain an awareness that his fantasies were a means for expressing his underlying anger, anxiety, and fears. David symbolically came out of his hole in the ground to confront his anger and gain some control over it. He was also able to better integrate his fantasy life with reality. Through his transference

Figure 3-27

drawings, he was able to acknowledge his feelings of helplessness as well as his difficulties in establishing trusting relationships. He was then able to symbolically confront these fears and make them less overwhelming to him. Throughout the therapeutic process, he was able to recognize and acknowledge his maladaptive ways of coping. Although the final drawings still indicated a tendency towards escapism, anxiety, and some depression, the final pictures were much less marked by his underlying anger, which presumably had been worked through.

4

Using Drawings in the Family System

THE FAMILY SYSTEM*

A family is a system composed of rules, communications, and hierarchies (Satir, 1967). All family systems are governed by rules that are either overtly or covertly stated and understood by all members. These rules determine the patterning of behavior and develop the homeostatic mechanisms that keep the family in balance. These mechanisms become triggered during a crisis to return the family to its previous equilibrium. For example, a mother may complain to the father who then argues with the son about his recent behavior. Father and son then quarrel, while mother withdraws from the situation. When this pattern is observed repeatedly, a family rule can be inferred, that is, resolution of disagreements between any dyad in this family

---

*Because of the complexity of family functioning and the need to have a working knowledge of family systems, this chapter will initially focus on theoretical aspects of the family before introducing drawing interventions.

is not acceptable. Despite the expressed concern regarding the identified patient's symptomatic behaviors on behalf of all family members, the family remains persistent in its attempt to maintain homeostasis, or the status quo, and will resist all efforts at changing the family structure. This makes the task of the family therapist extremely difficult.

NORMAL VERSUS DYSFUNCTIONAL FAMILY FUNCTIONING

In so-called "normal" functioning families, a homeostasis occurs when boundaries among members are clear, when there is flexibility in solving problems, when there is clear communication, and when there is no reinforcement for maladaptive behaviors. In contrast, dysfunctional families are exemplified by breakdowns in governing hierarchies, by unsuccessful attempts at problem solving, and by deficient reward exchanges. When dysfunctional, these patterns are the target of therapeutic change; when functional, they are the focus of support and strengthening (Minuchin, 1974).

There seems to be marked contrast in the subsystems (i.e., organized sections) of a family, between optimally competent families and those families that are less than efficient. A comparison between the two usually focuses on parental coalitions. These are usually found to be weaker in the dysfunctional family, where intimidation is seen instead of negotiation and hidden conflicts interrupt transactions between the members. In severely dysfunctional families, parental unity is fragile and leadership practically nonexistent, resulting in either dependent, clinging offspring who never leave home, or the oppositional child who leaves as soon as possible (Haley, 1980).

One way to learn about a family's functioning is to observe their coping strategies when a crisis arises. Some families learn by these setbacks, while others remain in their dysfunctional transactional patterns. To maintain effective relationships, families must establish and maintain clear channels of communication. If this does not occur, messages may be a "double bind," where contradictory or clouded messages confuse the receiver (Bateson, 1972). Additionally, when one member is scapegoated, he/she is often labeled the reason for family disharmony. When all focus is on this member, other sources of conflict among family members can be ignored.

Boundaries within the family structure become important statements when issues arise. Boundaries are invisible guidelines which define relationships among the family members (Gumaer, 1984). When underlying anger between spouses is displaced on the child, a comment has been made concerning limitations of participation. These predetermined roles are considered the family's boundaries. Boundaries can be viewed as being on a continuum from enmeshed to disengaged. An enmeshment occurs when boundaries among family members are blurred and members are overly involved. The concept of enmeshment includes such behaviors as constant interruption among family members or one family member always speaking for another. This often stifles growth and development. If an enmeshed family or couple continues to function in this manner, a separate sense of self is never learned or experienced. Of course, the opposite can occur when boundaries are too rigid, creating a wall of isolation and separateness. Thus, disengaged subsystems are perceived as low on interpersonal contact (Minuchin, 1974).

Families that function harmoniously are complex systems comprised of numerous segments, which interact in complicated arrays (Minuchin & Fishman, 1981). The subsystems of this group coexist within hierarchical structures with the distribution of power going from top to bottom. However, like most complex systems, there are linkages among the parts (or family members) that are stronger than the individual, no matter how powerful. Each family member belongs to several of these transactional units and plays distinct roles in each. The skills and rules for one subgroup may not be appropriate for another family subgroup. Within a functional family, the members are flexible to these changing roles and are adept at handling a variety of daily living situations.

THE ROLE OF THE MENTAL HEALTH PROFESSIONAL

The main target for the mental health professional is the family subsystems, which first must be delineated during a family evaluation. It is these dyads and triads that are the crux of the development of the family system and are the targets if changes are to occur. Recognition of this important aspect is critical for improving family functioning.

The family structure "frames" each member's identity within a social order (Minuchin & Fishman, 1981). In this organization lies a history of developing roles and unique perceptions which families bring into the therapeutic setting. Each member views him/herself as distinct from the other and as a part of a larger being from which they assess personal problems, strengths, and possibilities. (The case illustration at the end of this chapter emphasizes these separate and individual perceptions, as well as those of

111

the family as a group.) When families bring themselves to a professional third party, they are requesting an objective assessment of their particular reality which they have already "framed."

The initial goal for the evaluator then becomes to define and select those therapeutic truths that would benefit the family within their own problem-solving styles. During the evaluation process, obvious distinctions occur between the family's perception of their ongoing unit, which is trying to maintain itself, and the therapeutic stance of striving towards differentiation and competence among the family members. This creates a conflict from the start. In order to lead the family into an alternative structure or reality, the evaluator must enter into or "join" the family's reality, and vice versa. For example, if one of the father's roles in the family is to limit the family's disclosure to outsiders, the evaluator must connect with the father in such a manner as to get permission for interacting openly with other family members. Only later can the family therapist challenge this structure. Joining occurs when observations and respect for the family organization are made and when appropriate responses are given to all the members' unique realities.

PERFORMING FAMILY EVALUATIONS

In performing family evaluations, the clinician is provided with an abundance of information which must be filtered through strategic steps (Madanes, 1981; Minuchin & Fishman, 1981). There are boundaries to be observed, strengths to be emphasized, conflicts to be noted, and complementary patterns of functioning to be focused. Although the evaluator must always be generating hypotheses to be confirmed or ruled out, he/she must also prepare this process within an organized structure to facilitate change. The evaluator must arrange the information in such a way as to interrelate the facts and in such a manner that produces relevance for the primary therapist. A working plan or strategy that also details themes and goals thus becomes paramount.

As an initial working hypothesis regarding subgroup affiliations, it becomes important to corroborate or dismiss impressions about the family dynamics. This allows the clinician to begin intervening in the family structure. The observant evaluator will mentally note such aspects of the family as proximity of each member from one another, who speaks first or initiates most of the dialogue, who intrudes or talks for family members, who provides assistance, and who supplies confirmation. These initial hypotheses provide clues to the evaluator about who is closest to whom and what aspects about the family are unique concerning affiliations or coalitions, that is, who is rescuing whom and for what reason. Initial hypotheses also provide clues about overinvolvements among the subgroups of the family structure – for example, enmeshed dyads or closed triads – and to what extent these communication patterns support the continuation of this particular family system.

During the session, the evaluator is also actively observing the dynamics among the family members and the general mood of the session. The parents and children are illustrating some of their daily actions, for example, how they talk to one another or how the parents discipline the children. The overall mood of the evaluative session may be one of reluctance or helplessness in the case of a forced interview, or it may be one of anger and punishment where a threat by the parent(s) is being carried out (e.g., after repeated failures of discipline the father takes the child to the "shrink").

It is also crucial for the evaluator to make mental notes of the relationships among adult members (e.g., father and mother-in-law). The hierarchy among the generations provides a clue to whatever disharmony may be present. It is important to ascertain if a parent or grandparent was "dragged" to the interview or if the family is united to present an amicable front, denying any and all problems. This latter situation often occurs when the interview is being forced by a third party, such as the school system or hospital.

Of course, while the evaluator is actively making conjectures, these must be kept as working or tentative hypotheses. If the evaluator makes quick judgments or believes that the family will not change, then he/she may not be able to assimilate alternate ideas. Assessing families is a guessing game that always has to be validated as the session progresses. It is also of significance that the evaluator not share his/her observations or intrude in the family system at this stage since overinterpretation would be threatening and arouse unnecessary suspicions surrounding the need for treatment.

The mental health professional who performs family evaluations must obtain an abundance of knowledge about a family's dynamics in a very short time. He/she has the opportunity to learn communication patterns and secrecy among family members and to discover coalitions and splits within the family system. In order to accomplish this large task, he/she must pay particular attention to such things as:

1) Does the family member being addressed act politely or angrily?
2) Is the parent(s) talking about the child as if he or she didn't exist?
3) Does the parent appear concerned or worried?
4) Has the family participated in therapy before?
5) Do the family members have hope for successful change or do they feel helpless?
6) Who blames whom?
7) How do members react to disagreements or do they always all agree?
8) How is the identified patient behaving, i.e., is he or she upset? uncaring? and so on.
9) Is the parent really addressing his/her spouse when he/she talks about the child who has become the problem?

All these questions need answering before effective treatment can occur.

FAMILY ART EVALUATIONS

Generally speaking, the introduction of drawings into the family session gives the clinician an alternative way of observing family interactions. As a nonverbal approach, the use of drawings tends to bypass defenses by family members and promotes freer expression (Rubin, 1978). Drawings provide a "medium" for sharing family perceptions which are beyond the everyday experiences of the members. Some possible reasons why drawings may be used by the clinician to evaluate behaviors of the family are: 1) to gain new information through exposure to a novel experience; 2) to make goals for future interventions more concrete; 3) to disrupt maladaptive ways of communicating among family members; 4) to explore the alliances (i.e., dyads or triads) that may be inhibiting family functioning; 5) to enhance relationships through joint drawings; and 6) to aid, in a nonthreatening way, the expression of feelings.

Another advantage to introducing drawings into the family evaluation is that their use can equalize age differences. For example, parents tend to be more sophisticated verbally, whereas children generally feel more comfortable with concrete activities. Also, differences in the way family members express themselves through drawings may support changes in the usual roles of the family hierarchy and encourage flexibility in the way the members interact with one another (Wadeson, 1980).

In a "problem solving" approach to therapy, the therapist may use drawings to disrupt the existing family system by requesting role changes in the execution of the drawings. In this manner, the family can experience and practice these different arrangements within a rather safe environment. Drawings can also be used to help maintain balance once the family system begins to change (Landgarten, 1981).

When communication is focused on a shared product it is usually easier to encourage participation. During this time, the evaluator is able to acquire varied sources of diagnostic material (i.e., verbal, nonverbal, individual, and interactional) by carefully observing the family's behavior during the execution of drawings. The product's form and the family's associations to their products also provide the therapist with a wealth of information to generate initial working hypotheses.

Family dynamics are revealed in drawings through content, symbols, quantity, size, placement, process, and execution (Rubin, 1978). Roles and ways of communicating within the family structure are discovered by observing who leads or follows, who is assertive or passive, who is resistant, and so on. For example, role reversal may be evident in the family whose youngest member chooses the subject for the drawing and/or initiates the drawing. Withdrawn or shy family members may choose to work in the corner of the paper by themselves. Family members who are being "scapegoated" may get blamed for everything judged wrong in the drawing. Alliances and coalitions are often revealed in the placement of individual contributions to mutual drawings. A specific dyad within a family may be observed when two members work close together on the drawing. Conflicts between family members may be indicated when one family member consistently marks through another member's area of the drawing.

The art product can also reveal underlying messages and/or family secrets. Symbols used by individual family members often address such issues as what or who is important to them and how they relate to other family members. For instance, two family members who use the same symbol may be offering a clue about their allegience to one another within the family configuration. Destructive tendencies towards family members may be observed during the drawings – for example, when judgmental, rigid parents become critical of their child's work and attempt to redo it. Destructive tendencies can also be seen when the child continually seeks approval for his or her drawing and never obtains it. From these observations, hypotheses concerning family enmeshment or lack of nurturance may be generated for future validation.

The amount of time taken by a family to complete a drawing also may be of importance. The family who takes a long time to finish may be resistant to disclosing information about themselves and/or may be displaying their lack of trust in the therapeutic process. Further explanations regarding family dynamics revealed in drawings will be outlined in the case illustration at the end of this chapter.

Interpretations of drawings are only made after the family has been seen long enough for the clinician to recognize consistent symbols, patterns in execution, and so forth. As in verbal therapy, a certain amount of trust between the clinician and family must be established before interpretations can be effective. Thus, interpretations definitely are not made initially, as they may be too premature and inaccurate or insulting to the family which might jeopardize any future therapeutic involvement (Landgarten, 1981). In family art evaluations recommendations based on interpretations are usually made exclusively to the referring clinician. It is not helpful to interpret drawings for the family in these cases, but general recommendations to be given to the referring clinician can be shared with the family.

ADDING DRAWING DIRECTIVES TO MARITAL EVALUATIONS

Drawings may also be helpful in marital evaluations. Harriet Wadeson (1980) describes five advantages for using art in marital sessions. One is the "immediacy of doing a task together." Second, she states that the "genuineness" of unexpected material revealed in pictures may challenge old assumptions or beliefs which the couple has held onto firmly. Another advantage, according to Wadeson, is the "spatial expression" of pictures, which can symbolically reveal the couple's life space. The fourth advantage she describes is "permanence," whereby the drawing provides a concrete object to study, react to, use for clarification, and review. Finally, Wadeson describes the advantage of "shared pleasure." Picture making can become like a game to the couple who no longer find themselves having fun together.

There are three major drawing directives that are helpful in marital evaluations, according to Wadeson (1980). One is the "joint picture." The couple is instructed to draw a picture together, preferably without talking. Another helpful directive would be to ask the couple to construct individual abstract drawings to represent their relationship. Afterwards they are requested to draw a self-portrait to be exchanged with their spouse. This portrait should be a full figure and realistic. When completed, they give their drawing to their spouse. The clinician then gives them permission to amend the drawing of their spouse. These drawings often reveal such aspects of the relationship as which partner is the more dominant, the kinds of conflicts and power struggles being expressed, and the degree of intimacy.

Figures 4-1 and 4-2 were completed by a husband and wife during an initial consultation. Each had his/her own individual therapist and was becoming more and more estranged from the other. The couple was requested to make separate individual abstract drawings to represent each one's perceptions of the relationship.

The husband's drawing (see Figure 4-1) was an abstract depiction of a setting sun (encompassing everything) with mountains, birds, and trees in the foreground. He related that this was to symbolize the ideal nature of the couple's relationship prior to their problems. The clock on the left, which appeared to be melting, was an attempt at expressing his feeling that their relationship might not have much time left. The wife, from the same directive, drew three hearts – the one on the top right was the husband's, the one on the top left was hers, and the one below represented their daughter's (see Figure 4-2). She apparently saw their relationship as a carnival (the title). Later in the session she described it as a charade, stating that neither she nor her husband was being honest with each other. It was interesting to speculate (and later confirmed) that the black line representing the streamers actually separated her drawn heart from her husband's and daughter's, which was possibly her unconscious wish. With these drawings completed, the couple was able to begin talking more fully about their painful perceptions of the marriage.

Figures 4-3 and 4-4 followed from the directive to a couple to draw self-portraits then exchange them with the spouse. This couple had entered a local mental health clinic after each discovered that the other was having an extramarital affair. They were willing to attempt a reconciliation through marital counseling. In the first drawing completed by the wife, she, to the husband's surprise, entitled her portrait, "The Lonely Woman." In contrast, the wife was not surprised by her husband's self-portrait, which showed him in his work clothes. This apparently was her main complaint, that is, he was always working, which caused most of her loneliness.

When the counselor asked the couple to exchange drawings and amend them at their own discretion, the wife added another figure to represent her husband in more casual attire (see Figure 4-3). To her, this

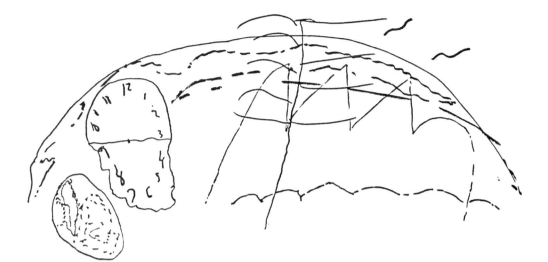

Figure 4-1

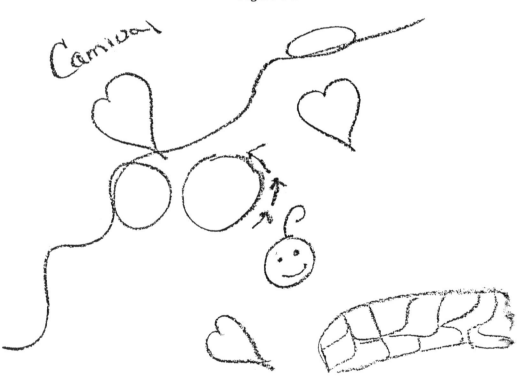

Figure 4-2

picture of her husband reminded her of happier times before they were married. The husband, in turn, changed his wife's self-portrait by emphasizing her mouth (see Figure 4-4). He turned the corners up into a smile and added the words "Discuss, discuss." Later in the session he revealed that he wanted his wife to talk to him more. According to him, even when he was available to his wife, she would only withdraw from his attempts at relating, making him feel frustrated and helpless. For many reasons they could not break this cycle of hurting the other and, upon realizing this through their drawings and verbal exchanges, continued to pursue a resolution of their problems through this style of counseling.

Figure 4-3

INTRODUCING DRAWINGS INTO FAMILY EVALUATIONS

If a clinician plans to use drawings when children or extended family come, a room large enough to accommodate all family members comfortably is needed. There also should be a table and/or easels, and drawing media. Hanna Kwiatkowska (1978), a pioneer in family art evaluations, has suggested that easels be arranged in a semi-circle so that family members can work independently and/or have the opportunity to view each other's

The Lonely Woman

Figure 4-4

work. If the clinician works in this fashion, it is best to include an extra easel to see who might isolate him/herself or place him/herself closer to a particular family member, which is pertinent to the identification of family alliances. It is best to include all family members if possible. Even children as young as age 3 or 4 can use art materials! Kwiatkowska (1978) has stated that an average time of 90 minutes to 2 hours is preferable for a proper evaluation session to allow for production of all drawings.

It should be noted that the introduction of drawings is not always well received and can be used defensively by the family. For example, the outstanding art skills of an individual family member may make other family members feel self-conscious. Often the entire family will be resistant initially. Hesitancy to engage in an evaluation is always evident to a certain degree, but it may be exacerbated when the family is faced with the novel situation of a joint art experience. While some authors believe that explanations usually arouse more anxiety (Kwiatkowska, 1978), others (e.g., Rubin, 1978) suggest that the clinician should attempt to explain the purpose of the evaluation and invite questions to reduce initial nervousness. In either case, clinicians need to be firm but supportive, and respectful towards the family, while reassuring them that their artistic skills are not being judged. Most of the time, it seems best to go ahead with the session, only spending time to deal with anxiety if it manifests itself as resistance and inhibits progress.

In most evaluations using drawings, members are asked to title, sign, and date their work. These actions tend to provide some closure on the particular session and aid in future reevaluations. Titles can be very revealing in terms of relevance to subject, "idiosyncratic" meaning, and degree of concreteness or additional symbolism. Often a title adds meaning to the picture for both the individual and the other participants. The size and placement of the signature may also be indicative of the individual's self-perception (Kwiatkowska, 1978).

ESTABLISHED FORMATS

There are several different formats presently used by therapists who use drawings for evaluation purposes. The authors of this book borrow many ideas from these noted art therapists when performing family art evaluations and revise them according to the various situations encountered. For example, a particular family may need to "see" their dynamics before accepting an interpretation, or another family may be resistant to discussing issues and drawings may "break the ice," or still another family may need something very concrete, such as a drawing, to define goals more readily. The mental health professional who adopts these approaches may want to modify them to his/her own unique style and setting. Parts or all of the entire drawing sequence can be an extremely helpful guide in which to interact and plan family sessions.

Discussions centered around shared art products generally follow principles of group therapy (see following chapter on groups). The evaluator's role is largely passive except in formats such as Landgarten's, in which the clinician tends to be more directive (Landgarten, 1981). The evaluator accepts all pictures and attempts to be nonjudgmental. He/she also encourages spontaneous discussion and facilitates the exchange of questions regarding each drawing among the family members (Kwiatkowska, 1978). Leading questions by the therapist may serve as a model for enhanced communication and help develop greater insight by the family. Examples of these types of questions might be: "Who was the leader?" "Who did the least?" "What emotions did you experience?" "Is the way in which you executed mutual work similar to the way you function at home?"

Kwiatkowska (1978) and Rubin (1978) tend to utilize a psychodynamic model when using drawings with families. Kwiatkowska instructs the family to complete six different drawings. The first is a "free picture" in which each family member is asked to draw whatever comes to mind. Often an individual member uses this drawing to introduce him/herself or to reveal certain aspects of the family problem.

A "free drawing" was completed by a mother who had entered the first of two art evaluation sessions upon the request of the family therapist who was a social worker (see Figure 4-5). In constructing this drawing she related the stress she was experiencing and the rest she was so yearning. She was a single mother with two daughters, ages 15 and 7. The older daughter, who was also drawing in the session, had recently entered a residential treatment center due to running away and truancy.

According to Kwiatkowska, family members are then asked to draw a picture of their family including themselves. (During this process, the family is encouraged to use whole figures).

In Figures 4-6 and 4-7, a daughter, age 16, and her mother, age 36, have drawn two different versions of their family. The daughter focused only on the immediate family members (from the left – mother, herself, a younger brother, then a younger sister) (see Figure 4-6), while the mother included her extended family (her mother and sisters), whom she depended upon (see Figure 4-7). Another striking difference in these two drawings was the

Figure 4-5

Figure 4-6

Figure 4-7

placement of the son. While the daughter had included him within the immediate family drawing, the mother placed him outside of the family configuration (bottom right) since he was living with the estranged father. These differences stimulated much discussion later with the primary therapist, a psychiatrist.

The third drawing in Kwiatkowska's sequence is an "abstract family portrait." This drawing allows the therapist to assess each person's ability to abstract. For families who do not understand the principle of abstraction, the clinician might direct them to do a drawing using "color, motion, lines, and shapes" to represent each family member.

A 15-year-old girl completed this "abstract family portrait" during a family evaluation (see Figure 4-8). This particular girl had begun to abuse drugs and skip school which led to the referral for an evaluation. This girl's

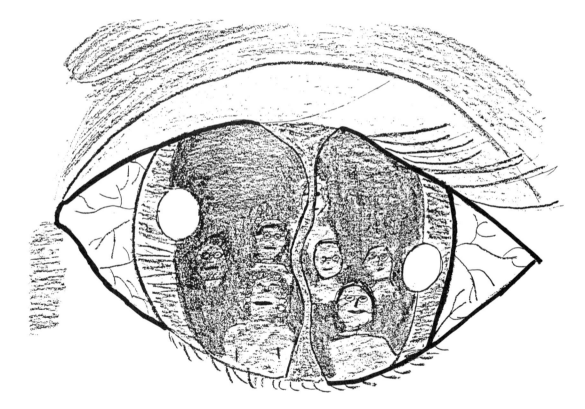

Figure 4-8

perception of her family, all encompassed within a huge eye, was certainly striking and probably indicated her desire for control. It was interesting to speculate on the wavy line she included down the middle of the eye, as an apparent split did exist within her family. The left side of the family in the drawing was darker and more clearly defined, which seemed to suggest she perceived them as being the more dominant members and their roles being less confusing. It was most significant that the figure caught in the middle was herself as she freely admitted feeling pulled from both sides.

The fourth picture in Kwiatkowska's sequence is started with the help of a scribble. Members are asked to do arm exercises (e.g., vertical, horizontal, and circular) using their whole body. They are then asked to scribble in the air and transfer this motion onto paper. The resulting scribble drawing is then made into a picture based on their individual projections and/or associations. This drawing is very similar to the scribble drawing sometimes used in individual evaluations (see Chapter 2 on assessment). However, the evaluator must consider that its content may be influenced by the fact that family members are present during its execution. The fifth picture (a joint scribble) is executed by repeating the above directions. However, after the scribbles are completed, family members are asked to project onto each other's scribbles. As a group they choose one scribble for a joint picture and agree on its subject.

The joint scribble of Figure 4-9 was relevant to the primary therapist, a psychologist, in many areas and fostered many discussions around sharing space and romantic notions. The psychologist was able to observe part of the art evaluation and benefited greatly from this process. The drawing, accomplished by a mother and her teenage daughter, had several important segments. After both had completed separate scribble drawings, the daughter wanted the mother to come to her easel (her level). This was very important since the mother was a much more sophisticated and controlled person. The mother had a very difficult time sharing space with the daughter since she herself was an artist highly critical of stray lines. (This also seemed to be a bone of contention within the household where the mother was well organized and the daughter a bit messy). After the mother finished the top part (a buzzard), the daughter stuck to the bottom, not daring to cross the midline. Her contributions, the word "Love" and what appeared to be an eye in the buzzard's stomach, created the impression with the therapist that romance and conception were a dominant concern with this girl. A month later it was learned that this girl, a 15-year-old, was pregnant.

The sixth and final picture in the family art evaluation, as espoused by Kwiatkowsa, is another "free drawing." The sequence of these six drawings

Untitled

Figure 4-9

initially gives family members more freedom of expression, provides some relaxation from tension with arm movements and scribbles, and permits access to their tolerance for stress.

By contrast, Rubin (1978) includes only three major tasks in her evaluation format. She begins with an individual picture done from a scribble. She asks each member of the family to draw a "continuous line" scribble. When finished they are asked if they "see" anything in their scribbles and to elaborate on them. Finally, they title them and share their work. The second drawing is a "family portrait" (abstract or realistic) which is again followed by sharing among the family members. The third drawing is a "joint mural" on 3′ × 6′ paper taped to the wall. This collaborative endeavor usually reflects the family's way of making decisions and interacting and should be carefully observed. If any family member should complete the first two tasks before other family members, they are asked to do a "free" product. The sequence in Rubin's format was designed to provide the most information with the least amount of stress. For example, the scribble drawing completed initially often reduces the family's anxiety and is an excellent tool for diagnosing individual, as well as family problems.

Landgarten's approach to evaluation differs in the philosophical stance from the two already mentioned (Landgarten, 1981). Her ideas on how to uncover the most information during an evaluation and prepare the family for treatment are rooted in "family systems theory," which emphasizes the influence that family members have on one another. Landgarten's main emphasis is not on the identified patient; rather, it is on the entire family. The family's behavior is observed through "problem solving" art tasks. The healthy family can accomplish these tasks without much difficulty, while signs of a dysfunctional family can be observed when coalitions begin to occur across levels of the family hierarchy during the evaluative process.

Landgarten first instructs family members to draw their initials as large as they can, and then to find a picture in them, to elaborate on them, to title their picture, and, finally, to share it with other family members. Like most projective techniques, the resulting drawing can reveal aspects of the individual's personality to the knowledgeable professional. In the second drawing, family members work together on a single piece of paper. They are not allowed to talk since nonverbal tasks usually elicit more unconscious material. Family members are asked to use different colored markers so individual contributions can be easily identified. If there are more than four or five family members, the directive is to divide the family into teams to draw separate pictures. At that time, much information is gained if the evaluator notes how the teams are formed.

128

A mother and her son called into a family therapy clinic for an emergency evaluation. The parents had recently separated, with the father leaving town. During the intake interview the mother expressed her exasperation in attempting to reconstruct her and her son's lives. She spoke of the tension between them and of her son's increasing anger and out-of-control behaviors. The son was beginning to have behavioral difficulties in his school and also was accused of setting fires.

As part of the comprehensive evaluation at the clinic the mother and her son, who by that time were not talking to one another, were requested to draw their initials as large as they could on a piece of paper and make it into a picture. The mother, whose initial was "A," constructed a house out of the letter (see Figure 4-10). Her use of the color red and the great amount of smoke coming out of the chimney indicated the possibility of much underlying anger, which she confirmed. The compulsively drawn bricks probably suggested her attempts at controlling the anger. The son's anger and need to control it could be seen from his attempt at making a drawing from his initial "O" (see Figure 4-11). His excessive use of red (the star and circle) and the thickness of the outer circle along with the placement of the drawing on the bottom were both indicators of the intensity of his emotion and need. His filling of the inner space with black probably addressed his inner experience of sadness. By using these drawings as a platform, the mother and son soon began to give each other permission to ventilate their many frustrations.

COMBINING STRATEGIC FAMILY THERAPY WITH ART

Another major proponent of family art evaluations, Sobol, has integrated strategic family therapy methods with art therapy techniques by using art tasks to elicit metaphorical information, alter family hierarchy and alliances, and increase self-exploration (Sobol, 1982). She utilizes the artwork metaphorically as a nonverbal communication task. For her, Jay Haley's concept of metaphor as basic to a family's communication was the link between the strategic model and art therapy (Haley, 1963). Art *is* metaphorical. Through artistic expression, the family can often represent problems in a more genuine manner and in a less destructive way then through words or actions (Sobol, 1982).

Information obtained from the art products is used to set goals and plan directives for the primary therapist. "Restructuring" of the family system is accomplished through the art task itself. Three kinds of art assignments have been mentioned by Sobol (1982). These include:

1) eliciting metaphorical information that can be used for planning future interventions – for example, interpreting a family member's drawing as representing his/her dominance and addressing that person with greater respect, or engaging the weaker member to allow that person to become a more active participant;

2) providing drawing tasks to interrupt the hierarchical sequences or intervene in the family coalitions (e.g., allowing the parents to work on a drawing without interruptions by their children); and

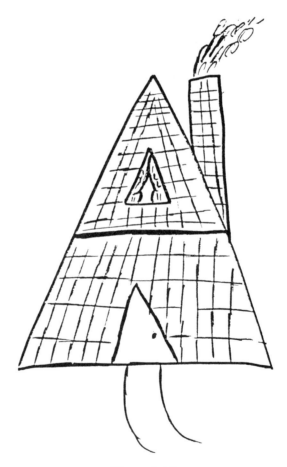

Figure 4-10

130

3) helping a particular family member to express him/herself through the drawing process, with an example being a younger, frustrated child who is not being "heard" by the rest of the family.

The co-author of this book who is an art therapist (Patricia Gould) became interested in the work of Sobol and integrated her use of therapeutic drawings within the framework of Haley's initial interview for evaluation purposes. According to Haley, four sequences usually occur during an initial interview (Haley, 1976). These include: 1) a "social" or greeting stage where everyone is welcomed and provided for in a comfortable manner; 2) a "problem" stage during which the therapist guides the family in elaborating on the immediate area(s) of concern; 3) an "interactive" sequence in which communication is established among the family members; and 4) a "goal-setting" phase where the family is requested to provide direction for therapeutic change. Haley also suggests homework tasks to keep the family

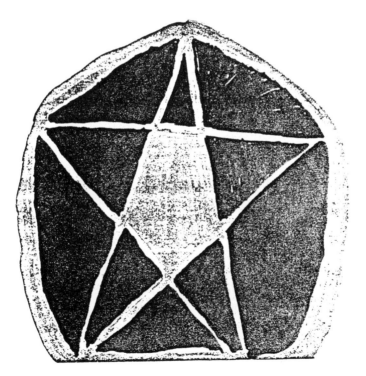

Figure 4-11

131

involved. This is easily accomplished with directives for simple art tasks to be done at home.

A possible art task for the social stage might be simply to ask family members to construct a free drawing. It might also be possible to combine the social and problem stages with directives such as "Do a drawing to represent why you think you are here," or "Do a drawing to represent the problem." To help establish the family's goals, the clinician might ask family members to do individual drawings of how they would like to see the problem changed. For the interaction stage the therapist could ask each member to "Draw how you see the family" and to do a joint mural which allows the clinician to focus on family systems. It is at this stage that the clinician could further evaluate the family by specifically asking the previously observed dyads or triads in the family to work together. The ending stage is used for review of drawings. The following case illustration exemplifies how various drawing directives can be used to accomplish the stages of Haley's initial interview.

CASE ILLUSTRATION

The Budd family was referred for evaluation purposes because their 17-year-old son, Tom, had been court ordered for psychiatric hospitalization after having stabbed his 12-year-old sister, Amy. Tom denied any memory of the incident and attributed the event to drug and alcohol abuse. The hospital treatment team had observed only mild behavioral pathology during Tom's evaluative period on the adolescent unit, and his individual psychological and neurological tests did not disclose significant aberrations. The referring physician requested additional information from the unit social worker concerning the family's functioning to aid in determining whether a return home for Tom was a possibility. The Budd family had been referred to a strategic family therapist in the community who would see them when Tom was released from the hospital. Because the family had been extremely guarded and defensive towards the social worker during her intake telephone interviews, she decided to use family drawings as a nonthreatening vehicle to break through the family resistance during her initial meetings. (The social worker had previous training in family art evaluations and often worked in conjunction with an art therapist when performing family evaluations). Recommendations based on interpretations of the family drawings were to be forwarded to the treatment team as well as to the community family therapist.

Mr. and Mrs. Budd and Amy came to the hospital for these evaluation sessions. Mrs. Budd appeared to be "the authority" and dominant member of this family configuration. She repeatedly made statements about how "open" the family was and how willing they were to help Tom "fix his problem." During the initial drawing segments, she also tended to explain the drawings completed by other family members as well as deny or disqualify their observations.

The family was seen five times for this segment of the family evaluation where drawings were used as the main vehicle of expression. These sessions lasted from 1-1½ hours. The family members were asked to separately draw: 1) how they saw "the problem"; 2) how they would like to see "the problem" changed; 3) how they viewed their lives before, during, and after "the problem"; and 4) a picture of their family. They were then asked to draw a mural together and then do another joint mural with the father as leader. In addition, a dual picture was requested of the mother and father.

The initial drawing by daughter Amy revealed her nervousness surrounding the unusual environment within the family therapy room (i.e., one-way mirror, microphones, etc.). In the picture she included the microphones hanging from the ceiling and the camera window in the upper right-hand corner (see Figure 4-12). This picture had an intrusive quality, perhaps symbolically reminiscent of the fear experienced in the evaluation process, or possibly reflecting the intrusiveness later established within the family system. It is also possible that this theme could be a symbolic reflection of the feeling of being stabbed. The black heavy line enclosing the room probably represented her need to contain her anxious feelings. In fact, the entire family seemed to have a primary need for control as indicated by their choice of art media available to them, i.e., their selection of pencil and marker. This was probably a sign that all family members were experiencing a high level of anxiety.,

In contrast, Tom's initial drawing seemed to reflect more directly his concern regarding "the problem" (see Figure 4-13). The black cloud over his head seemed to suggest his underlying depression, or possibly the uncertain future, and the ropes attached to his body his feelings of helplessness. His encircled thoughts included symbols for several areas of concern, that is, alcohol, drugs, cars, girlfriend, job, and school grades.

The first drawing by the father revealed a considerable degree of anxiety as indicated by the sketchy line quality and the many erasures (see Figure 4-14). In comparison to the other family members, his drawing was rather empty, reflecting his lack of spontaneity and constricted affect. Inter-

133

estingly, the only color in the drawing, red, was placed inside the house, possibly suggesting his perception of a volatile household situation. Both parents, however, tended to deny the existence of any problems within the family. The father's denial was further strengthened in the subject matter of his drawing. He drew the son, Tom, coming home rather than as a source of any problem. He also described himself and his drawing as "dumb," revealing his low opinion of himself and his perceived lack of importance to the family.

Drawings of how the family would like to see the problem changed were generally idealized. For example, Amy's drawing as dictated by this directive illustrated that Tom's problems were simply overlooked or "crossed

Figure 4-12

out" by everyone (see Figure 4-15). Often, "crossing out" objects in drawings is an overt indicator of denial. In addition, no one at that point in the evaluation was accepting any responsibility for the problem. The mother's dominant role in the family and her tendency to deny the problem were illustrated by her statement "our happy family" and the house containing the words "Home Sweet Home." The use of denial in the drawings by both mother and daughter also indicated the close emotional bond between mother and daughter.

Conflict between the parents became evident in Mrs. Budd's "before, during, and after" drawing (see Figure 4-16). In all stages of the drawing she emphasized her husband as leaving or absent and portrayed herself as having to complete tasks she felt should have been done by him.

Figure 4-13

Figure 4-14

Figure 4-15

Figure 4-16

The house in the father's attempt at "before, during, and after" drawings changed considerably throughout this assignment (see Figure 4-17). In the "before" segment of the drawing the entire house was filled with the color red, while the "during and after" portions were only partially drawn in red. It is possible that more anger and turmoil were experienced within the household before the incident, and that the actual stabbing and repercussions may have relieved some of this perceived pressure. The stabbing incident may also have been viewed as a metaphor for the father's anger

Figure 4-17

and the possibility that the son had acted out the father's conflict towards his wife. It also became evident in the drawing that the father felt that his son was feeling overwhelmed by working too much, which was also a feeling shared by the rest of the family towards him. In the "before" portion of the drawing, Tom's employer was asking him to work, while his school principal was telling him that his grades were poor. Mr. Budd also indicated through the drawing that he felt unavailable to Tom during this time by showing himself going off to work. The father's attempts to align himself with Tom were also revealed in this drawing by the addition of the black cloud in the middle section. (Tom's previous two drawings had included a black cloud).

It was important to note that although the entire family verbally expressed their desire to have Tom home, a more accurate reflection of their underlying ambivalence was revealed in their drawings. This was especially true in the above drawing by the father in addition to his initial drawing of the problem. This theme was also repeated in his second drawing of "how he would like to see the problem changed" (see Figure 4-18). In all of these drawings, he consistently placed Tom at a "safe" distance from the rest of the family.

Amy's "before, during, and after" drawing revealed a secret she had not told anyone prior to the sessions (see Figure 4-19). At the beginning she drew herself wondering whether she should tell her mother that Tom had started drinking. Apparently, she knew Tom kept his "booze" in the basement (where the stabbing occurred) and had been threatening to tell on him.

Other drawings by the family again revealed their tendency to use denial as their major defense and to portray themselves as a happy family without problems. Mr. Budd's family portrait showed him and his wife overseeing the garden and Tom and Amy playing ball and riding bikes (see Figure 4-20).

Figure 4-18

Two examples of the family's joint murals illustrate the difference between an undirected mural (see Figure 4-21) and one in which the examiner positioned the father as the leader to support him in being more involved with the family (his previous artwork had suggested that he was the parent who was least involved) (see Figure 4-22). It is important to note that the family's artwork in these murals consistently overlapped, indicating their lack of clear boundaries, which is suggestive of an enmeshed family.

Figure 4-19

Figure 4-20

Figure 4-21

In Figure 4-21 , Mrs. Budd was the initiator and directed the drawing's entire execution. Mr. Budd drew only the trees along the top of the hill, the clouds, and the sun. In the end, he was working entirely alone. This again accentuated his peripheral role in the family constellation. The tree in the center, which was red in color, was one which Mrs. Budd had asked her husband to transplant. He refused this request, leaving her to do it alone. This again could be perceived as indicative of their conflict and their lack of cohesiveness in problem solving. Mrs. Budd drew Mr. Budd as a small figure next to the pool; Mr. Budd responded by adding a hat on his head, which is often considered a symbol of control. This was likely to have been a

Figure 4-22

142

symbolic attempt at controlling his anger towards her. Amy, the daughter, then hastily drew her mother next to the house, a "safe" distance from the father. Here she seemed to be playing a protective role in her parents' conflict. Mrs. Budd next drew the two children in the pool together. Amy responded by drawing herself splashing the water, almost as an immediate release of the anxiety she was probably experiencing when placed so close to the brother who had nearly killed her. Mr. Budd was the first member of the family to quit drawing, with Tom stopping shortly thereafter, again reemphasizing their need to align themselves against the two female figures. The mother and daughter remained involved in the drawing to add their finishing touches, with the mother drawing the house on the left and the tree on the right.

In the second drawing (see Figure 4-22), Mr. Budd initially exhibited appropriate leadership abilities by directing Amy to draw the hospital, Mrs. Budd the home, and Tom his school. Mr. Budd connected the three places with a road. It was not long after this that the family excluded the father and he resorted to asking them what they were doing. Eventually, he resumed his peripheral role by adding the clouds and the sun.

In discussing the mural, Mrs. Budd supported her husband in taking a more active role and becoming more involved at home. He responded by emphasizing that the home was the mother's "jurisdiction" and work was his, thus indirectly supporting her status.

Finally, the examiner requested that the mother and father draw together while the children observed. This was done to gain further information regarding the parents' conflict and their children's role in it. The examiner had hypothesized that this task would most likely be particularly difficult for the parents to accomplish, but it would clarify their differences.

Mrs. Budd started drawing without consulting Mr. Budd and resisted his ideas and attempts to draw. They then had an argument over the appropriate colors to use. Tom repeatedly intervened and attempted to make helpful suggestions even though the therapist had requested that he not speak. This minor episode certainly appeared to be an accurate reflection of the family system and the anxiety created once the parents began to fight.

To further illustrate this point, a drawing completed during Tom's individual art therapy sessions has been included (see Figure 4-23). Tom portrayed himself drowning in the water between two separate piers where his parents were standing. His mother was pictured trying to save him, while his father felt that he could make it on his own. It would seem that his mother was fostering his continued dependence while his father was supporting his independence. Another possible interpretation might be to perceive the differences between the two in caring for Tom. Whichever, it was this "bind" that Tom graphically symbolized of his separation/individuation struggle for an identity which seemed to be an ongoing issue for him.

Based on the content of this family's artwork and their observed behavior during their attempts, it seemed that the conflict between the parents was a primary source of anxiety within the family and a place to begin exploring in family therapy, which was recommended. Mr. Budd appeared angry but ineffectual in coping with this anger by withdrawing which maintained his state of frustration. Although Mrs. Budd appeared frustrated with her husband's lack of family involvement, she seemed to support his withdrawal to keep her status by ignoring or criticizing his attempts at asserting himself. This "bind" certainly seemed to have a significant impact on the children who appeared sensitive to this conflict between their two sources of nurturance. In the end, it may have been Tom's way of symbolically acting out his

Figure 4-23

father's anger and relieving his own internal stress by aggressively attacking his sister.

After this evaluative period, the parents were seen by the social worker without the children for a period of time to work out their conflicts in order to present a stronger unit to their children. When Tom was released from the hospital, the strategic family therapist at the local health department continued the work of strengthening the family hierarchy. This seemed to reduce much stress within the family and they were able to become more flexible in dealing with their daily problems. Eventually, Tom graduated from high school and secured a job out of town with the help of a relative.

5

Using Drawings in Group Treatment

USING GROUP APPROACHES IN TREATMENT*

Almost all mental health professionals will at one time or another use group approaches in their everyday milieu for a variety of populations and for a variety of reasons. Whether on an inpatient, a day treatment, or an outpatient basis, therapists often are required to form and facilitate groups. Some types of approaches that are commonly employed include those using theoretical orientations (e.g., psychoanalytic or insight-oriented groups, gestalt, rational-emotive) or those groups formed to remediate specific problem areas (e.g., social skills deficits, stress, drug or alcohol abuse). Leaders of groups utilize an array of both verbal and nonverbal techniques

---

*The significance of introducing drawings into the group process will be the primary emphasis in this chapter and will be detailed in later sections. First, however, it is necessary to gain an understanding of the principles and theories of group dynamics.

and directives, in addition to structured exercises. These techniques might include reflection and clarification, for example, or introduce more active approaches such as role playing.

Groups serve preventive as well as remedial purposes (Corey, 1981). Although groups may have a specific focus such as vocational or educational, they also encompass interpersonal processes that emphasize thoughts, feelings, and behavior. Groups are also largely problem-oriented, wherein the participants may be confronting situational and/or temporary struggles or minimizing self-defeating behaviors. The group provides the empathy and support required by each member. These, in turn, establish an environment of trust which culminates in the sharing of conflicts and the opportunity to investigate these concerns.

Essentially, the role of the group leader is to act as facilitator of the interactions among participants. This facilitative role aids the participants in broadening their knowledge and awareness of one another and in helping to specify personal goals and actions for a relief of symptoms. This reliance on group members to provide acceptance and direction is the main difference between group psychotherapy and individual psychotherapy, where the therapist functions as the primary change agent (Yalom, 1970).

GOALS OF GROUP THERAPY

Although group members decide the more specific goals of each group experience, some aspects of the goals are usually shared by all types of groups. These are: 1) learning to trust themselves and others; 2) recognizing the commonality of presented problems; 3) discovering alternative strategies in resolving conflicts; 4) increasing independence; 5) incorporating a larger repertoire of social skills; and 6) clarifying and modifying personal values (Corey, 1981).

There are many advantages to establishing therapeutic groups as a method for assisting individuals. They provide a major opportunity for participants to discover ways of relating to one another and to receive invaluable feedback on how others perceive and experience their presence. The therapeutic group in several ways recreates their everyday world and is a microcosm of their environment. The process throughout the group experience offers a sample of concerns which are little different from what people experience outside the group.

The group provides support and understanding to increase self-disclosure and the participants begin to achieve a sense of belonging which brings new insights. With this foundation, the participants are able to take more risks and explore alternatives to their self-defeating behaviors and practice new behaviors within an uncritical atmosphere. The complexities of individual psychotherapy become enhanced in group work, especially regarding the interrelationships and dynamics of the group as it progresses.

Yalom's *The Theory and Practice of Group Psychotherapy* has been considered the standard in compiling the theoretical foundations of the group experience (Yalom, 1970). He provides a list of "curative factors" in the process of group therapy which include:

1) Interpersonal input – i.e., group members providing feedback
2) Catharsis – i.e., gaining relief through verbalizing frustrations
3) Group cohesiveness – i.e., no longer having to feel alone
4) Insight – i.e., realizing unconscious reasons for behavior
5) Interpersonal output – i.e., engaging other people in conflicts
6) Existential awareness – i.e., acknowledging the uncertainties of life
7) Universality – i.e., learning the commonalities of all people
8) Instillation of hope – i.e., realizing the group can be of great benefit
9) Altruism – i.e., putting the needs of others first
10) Family reenactment – i.e., reliving experiences within the family
11) Guidance – i.e., gaining direction from group members
12) Identification – i.e., discovering a mentor from within the group

PLANNING FOR GROUP TREATMENT

For a successful group to occur, the therapist must plan thoroughly. This may constitute such efforts as: drafting a procedure which specifies the primary basis for establishing a group; detailing the kinds of participants to be involved; providing a selection process; estimating the size, frequency, and duration; concluding or considering whether the group will be open to volunteers or closed without changing members; and choosing some guidelines for follow-up and evaluating the efficacy of the group. This preparation phase is probably one of the most crucial steps in whether the group experience will be successful (Corey, 1981). Yalom proposes that cohesiveness (i.e., compatibility) is a key ingredient in the selection of group members

(Yalom, 1970). Thus, in selecting members, the leader(s) may want to ask who will most likely benefit from this type of experience and who will most likely disrupt the group if included.

The decision of whom to include in the group depends on a clear statement of purpose. The group may have as its focus a specific problem, (e.g., alcohol or drugs) where age may not make a difference, or it could focus on the problems common to a particular age (e.g., starting school), where a homogeneous age grouping is essential. A more varied group might be more appropriate when the focal point for the group is to receive feedback from diverse sources. The therapist must keep in mind that the nature of the population will also govern the characteristics of the group structure (Wadeson, 1980). For example, participants who are insight-oriented will most likely be willing to share more than verbally limited individuals. Or a more specific example might be a group of mothers of autistic children who will tend to focus on the special issues regarding the behavior of their children.

The membership and group size depend on the type of setting from where the selection is taking place, and, to a certain extent, on the experience of the leader. Also, the number included in the group is somewhat dependent on the amount of time allowed and the attention span of all group members. For example, the therapist may find it necessary to have the number of 7-year-old hyperactive boys to be fewer than a group of depressed adults. A group of hyperactive boys may be limited to 4 to 6 members, whereas the group of depressed adults may function better with as many as 10 members. Of course, ideal group members are the ones who are willing and able to express themselves verbally, and in the case where drawings are introduced, graphic communication becomes paramount.

The frequency of group meetings is also contingent on the type of group established. Typically once a week is the generally conceived format of most groups, although it may be better to schedule more frequent and shorter groups for children and early adolescents. The duration of the group should be clarified from the beginning. In this manner the members will have a clear idea of the plans and focus of the group structure.

STAGES OF GROUP PROCESS

After all is established, preparation and organization become essential for a successful group experience to occur. This may entail an exploration of the participants' expectations, fears, and so forth. Without this initial structure during the early phases of groups, the participants' worries will become magnified. During this exploratory time of the group, the participants' viewpoints become focused on getting accustomed to the rules, on learning everyone's concerns, on shaping the goals, and on searching for a niche within the group. It is in this phase that acting out to test limits will most likely occur. It is also a time for seeking an identity in the group and laying the basic foundation for establishing trust. This latter quality is especially important if the group is ever going to get past superficial interactions. When trust is established, more risk-taking, feedback, and experimentation will result as the group experiences more cohesiveness from within its membership.

Before a group begins working on individual and process problems, a phase usually occurs in which much defensiveness and resistance take place (Corey, 1981). This ambivalence, which is created by the conflict between wanting safety and security versus wanting to feel free and open, causes many struggles in the early stage. The effective group leader must attempt to acknowledge the anxieties that are being observed and respect this condition in order to increase participation. Another significant occurrence that begins to surface during this transitional step is characterized by conflicts surrounding dominance and control (Schutz, 1961; Yalom, 1970). This struggle for power is often displayed by negative comments, jockeying for leadership, rivalry for attention, and the establishment of a social pecking order. Throughout this discordant period, the group leader may also become challenged and criticized. For the leader, the most critical aspects of this phase are to intervene at appropriate times, to aid in recognizing and expressing anxieties, to be able to point out defensive postures, and to instruct participants in dealing with conflicts. By doing this, the leader will provide a comfortable environment, which will allow exploration, and influence the group in ways that will increase a sense of autonomy.

The substance of any group is found in its willingness to work on significant problems and the avenues it discovers to bring about noticeable resolutions with concomitant behavioral changes. It is at this juncture that crucial directions be taken by the leader to encourage independent decision making for exploring group issues; to help each participant become a significant member of the group and at the same time retain personal identity; and to allow feedback to filter through each participant, who must then decide on what to personally incorporate into his/her already existing belief system. This is when the group has become its own leader and the focus is on productivity. During this time, there is an acceptance of and caring for one another. This is also a time when there is a sense of hope and a belief that sought-after changes will occur, when plans of action are discovered, and when intimacy is accepted with a willingness to self-disclose, from which freedom of expression will result. When a group is truly functioning, the leader can relax and permit the group to do most of the work.

The final issue of any group is for the individuals to learn the ability of generalizing the new perceptions and new behaviors gained while in the group into their outside worlds. This is a time for reflection, summarizing, integrating, and interpreting the experience that occurred. This phase of termination will most assuredly leave a final impression on all participants and will be decisive in evaluating the success or failure of the group experience. If issues are left unresolved or if the participants are not willing to explore their new talents in their environment, failure and disappointment will most likely result. It is critical that the leader take an active role in these closing sessions. Topics to be discussed need to include: 1) feelings surrounding separation and loss; 2) reminders that the participants themselves were responsible for any accomplishments that may have occurred; 3) preparation for dealing with and effectively changing significant others outside of the group; 4) specification of actual gains derived from the encounter; 5) opportunity for providing and receiving final feedback from all group members (including the leader); and 6) clarification of unfinished business. For the leader, this final step means providing a format that will allow the participants a greater understanding of their experience and enhance positive transfer of new learning to novel surroundings.

ADVANTAGES OF INTRODUCING DRAWINGS
INTO GROUP TREATMENT

There are many reasons for introducing drawings into groups. Within acute inpatient settings or within crisis groups, drawings can be used to identify precipitating events that led to trauma or hospitalization. They can also be used to identify goals and used to achieve the stated goals. Adding graphic expression to verbal methods can extend awareness of conflicts, diminish reality distortion, and increase mastery over destructive behavior. Thus, by splitting therapeutic sessions into verbal and graphic sharing, the issues and reactions raised during the verbal sessions provide subject matter for artwork, and vice versa (Cardone, Marengo, & Calisch, 1982).

Drawings can also be used as a vehicle of communication in groups when the members seem to have trouble expressing themselves. This use has been demonstrated successfully in art therapy groups organized for mothers of autistic children (Stone, 1982). Drawings offer a concrete way of providing clarification for confusing thoughts and feelings. The finished product increases a sense of self-worth and accomplishment and helps build a foundation of self-esteem.

It is felt that the most important contribution in using drawings within the group format is the sharing of images, that is, the feeling of being known at a deep, personal level (Wadeson, 1980). Drawings also give structure to groups by providing a task as a concrete point of reference. In this way, the drawings can be focused on directly, and the participant indirectly, thus making interpretations less threatening.

The role of the therapist in groups that use drawings, as in traditional verbal groups, is to reflect or clarify the issues raised and to maintain a psychological climate of acceptance and understanding. Generally speaking, drawing directives from the therapist must provide suggestions and structure initially, much like the beginning of any group. The introduction of drawing directives enhances the development of verbal communication by initially providing a less threatening way of disclosing underlying feelings and conflicts. Self-disclosure in groups that use drawings, as in most traditional groups, may initially occur between the therapist and group member on an individual basis, but the therapist eventually tries to encourage it among all group members.

When drawings are used in group therapy, spontaneous expression is very much encouraged. However, the therapist must require nondestructive behaviors, that is, respect for art materials, no throwing (especially in children's groups), no destruction of artwork (except in isolated cases if it has some therapeutic value), and so on. Additionally, the therapist must encourage responsible behavior by requiring that members clean up materials after the sessions and return the materials to their original location. In this manner, participation and commitment are strongly emphasized. Drawings are kept by the therapist in a "safe" place as a way of establishing trust, transference, and so forth. Drawings are usually dated, signed, and titled for future displaying periodically by the therapist and for reference and review.

DRAWING DIRECTIVES USED TO DEFINE
AND ENHANCE THE GROUP EXPERIENCE

During the formative sessions of group therapy where drawings are used, there are likely to be definable stages. These include:

1) *Introduction to other group members and clarification of goals.* This can be accomplished through drawings by requesting self portraits, asking for symbols that represent problems/solutions, disclosing weaknesses, likes and dislikes, or possibly by drawing a circle with the instruction, "Fill your world." Other directives could include "Draw why you are here" or "Draw something you would like to change."

2) *Sharing with other group members.* This might entail passing around a beginning drawing and having the other group members finish it. Another possibility would be to allow the group to make a combined drawing on a large piece of paper tacked to the wall. By this time, the group usually has become more cohesive and the therapist has become less directive.

An example of this "sharing" stage was a drawing constructed by a group of artists. At an initial session they were requested to trace around their dominant hand, then to "fill it in, cut it out, and place it on a larger piece of paper together with the other group members' hands." In the beginning, placement of the hands was completed separately and apart from one another. When the group leader invited everyone to make changes, the participants began to move their drawn hands closer together, which produced a marked increase in nervousness. Their overall high level of anxiety and resistance in regard to sharing the work space appeared to manifest itself in the extremely shaky line quality and in the lack of containment. The group's behavior during the execution of the project was also indicative of anxiety as the members laughed and talked excessively. Some hesitancy was also suggested by the mural, as three group members worked on the outside.

3) *Revelation of participants' roles in the groups through their drawings.* The therapist is often able to determine the group dynamics through viewing certain key elements in the drawings. For example, the therapist notices the high frequency of marks drawn by an individual (probably the most dominant member), who may also tend to draw the large or centrally located objects in his/her drawings, or discovers the more ineffectual, withdrawn member, who may tend to place him/herself on the edges of the paper or who offers only minimal markings. Leaders within the group structure are usually revealed through asserting themselves by deciding what the group will draw or by providing more commands during the process of a group drawing. Those individuals who may likely try to sabotage the group are

154

often the ones who cross or mark through another member's drawings. It is helpful to the therapist if each group member uses a different color marker for identification purposes. The therapist can become more directive in developing insight regarding the group member roles by asking them to provide a drawing of how they see themselves in the group, or provide two separate drawings – one on how they see themselves and the other on how they imagine how others see them.

Figures 5-1 and 5-2 show how this group member sees himself as somewhat shy and uncertain, whereas he feels that others see him as angry.

Another directive for drawings that encourage group participation could be, "Draw how you see other members of the group." This one is

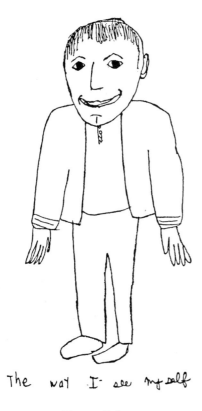

The way I see myself   the way others see me

Figure 5-1   **Figure 5-2**

somewhat riskier and may make group members feel more defensive. Therefore, this technique should only be used when the group has become more supportive of one another. Of course, group support is developed throughout the process and facilitated by the therapist's interventions and suggestions. An example that emphasizes this process may be the therapist instructing the members to "draw a symbol for a problem," coupled with passing it around for other group members to add their own "symbols" of support. Group discussions of the drawings are always encouraged throughout this process. It is also important periodically to allow free choice of the subject matter for drawings to foster independent functioning within groups and allow expression of issues that the therapist may not have addressed.

In Figure 5-3, we see an adolescent boy's view of himself with and without people. It is noteworthy that when he is alone he portrays himself drawing. In this particular case, his artwork may have been his protection. Because he happened to be adequate in drawing, however, it actually helped enhance his self-esteem in a group setting. The drawing also sug-

Figure 5-3

gested other hypotheses that could be explored further. For example, it could be that when this boy was with other people he became much more of a performer or a leader, or perhaps was more sure of the expectations surrounding his role.

Drawings need to be saved in separate portfolios throughout the group experience and are reviewed periodically, for example, at the end of a group or when a particular group member leaves. This provides closure for the group and/or participant and signifies changes that are happening in the group process. Some directives that might be appropriate for this end phase include:

1) Make three separate drawings – one of yourself at the beginning or before the group started, one of yourself during the group, and one of yourself at present.
2) Make drawings that represent another group member at the beginning and ending of the group.
3) Draw a memory of another "leaving" or "ending" in your life.
4) Draw the feelings you have about leaving this group.
5) Draw symbols for what you feel you got out of this group.
6) Draw your future goals beyond this group.

The drawing in Figure 5-4 represents a young adolescent boy's feelings in regard to leaving a therapeutic group experience. Through the drawing he revealed his inner turmoil surrounding the themes of loss and depression. At the same time he attempted to add his deeper fears that he would not be missed. His anger and low self-esteem were readily apparent by the highly charged statements within the drawing.

DRAWING DIRECTIVES USED FOR DIFFICULT PARTICIPANTS

During the group experience, the leader is likely to face a variety of common problematic individuals. The following descriptions include just a few types of difficult individuals the leader may encounter and possible strategies to use when utilizing art materials.

When faced with an isolated individual, 1) divide the group into pairs, then gradually increase the numbers involved in a particular drawing; 2) explore attitudes by having group members draw how they feel when they are with others and when they are alone; 3) begin by requiring drawings but not forcing verbal sharing initially.

For the aggressive, acting-out individual, the group leader might find it

157

worthwhile to reiterate the ground rule, which states that group participants are not allowed to destroy artwork. It should be stressed that drawings are important expressions of individuals and should be kept. However, if an individual does destroy his/her drawings, the pieces should be retrieved from the garbage, if necessary by the therapist, to emphasize the importance of not (symbolically) destroying and/or rejecting a part of themselves (i.e., their self-expression). Interpretation at that point may be helpful if the individual has developed any trust in the therapist. Ideally, this individual will be able to respond to directives by the therapist to draw a symbol for his/her anger, or scribble it out in a spontaneous, expressive manner. It should be emphasized that it is "OK" to express anger in this more appropriate manner.

It may also be possible to use group pressure from other participants to counteract the outburst of the aggressive member. Group support may be

Figure 5-4

158

elicited by the therapist requesting that all group members draw symbols of their anger. Sending an angry person out of the room is a last recourse and pursued only if he/she continues to be destructive. The group leader does not want any participant to feel rejected for being angry. If the angered participant chooses to become angrily defiant and withdrawn, he/she should be allowed to do so. However, the therapist should attempt to interpret his/her behavior and possibly have the rest of the group do drawings regarding how they might interpret his/her behavior. If this person is unable to express his/her anger symbolically and is consistently hindering the development of the group, only then should he/she be asked to leave.

When confronted with the typical exclamation ("I don't know how to draw!"), the therapist might indicate that this is not an art class and that he/she is not being judged on the art product; rather, any form of self-expression is acceptable. The participant who refuses to draw, like the isolated participant, could probably be helped in dual work. It is posssible that this individual has performance anxiety, is displaying defiance, and/or has possible fears of regressing, which the therapist may want to explore further. Any type of power struggle that may be created by this type of individual should try to be avoided. As always, a permissive, nonjudgmental supportive environment is helpful when attempting to diminish these problems.

When faced with an "anxious" participant who verbalizes excessively while others are trying to concentrate on drawings, it is often helpful to require drawings to be completed without talking. Whenever a participant begins "feeling stuck" (due possibly to his/her anxieties), it might be helpful to introduce free drawings or nonstructured, projectivelike drawings (e.g., the scribble technique) to provide the therapist with information with which to continue. Whenever it is likely that not all group members will finish their product on time, it is better to set a time limit. The dynamics surrounding which one of the participants rushes to finish first and/or who keeps the group waiting may be explored and a mental note made for future interpretation or feedback.

DRAWING DIRECTIVES USED FOR DIFFERENT AGE GROUPINGS

Another important concern in forming groups that use drawings in order to enhance interactions is age differences. Children through latency age (i.e., 6 to 9 years) often do not have insight into their drawings and are just beginning to learn how to work and interact socially with their peers.

With this in mind, the person in charge needs to appoint a leader when working with children rather than to allow a natural leader to emerge, which would be more appropriate for an older age group. Also in the younger group it is necessary to afford members the opportunity to exchange leadership roles to promote and teach social interaction.

Groups with young children must be more structured and task-oriented. The behavior during execution and the drawings themselves are observed carefully for underlying material. This information is used to meet therapeutic goals. For example, the therapist may observe a child who has problems with impulse control drawing quickly, becoming easily frustrated, and finishing with a messy product. The therapist could provide this type of child with the structure of simple tasks that gradually increase in complexity to enhance the development of controls. (Usually one can detect a younger child in a group with poor impulse control by merely viewing a completed mural. When this type of child is leading the group, the mural tends to be messier.)

Young children may graphically express problems they may be unable to express verbally, such as a problem at home between the parents, or being abused or neglected by the parent. With this age group it is often helpful to use drawings metaphorically to work through the fears stemming from these difficulties. For example, the therapist may recognize these fears when the child repeatedly draws monsters. The therapist may intervene in this case by suggesting the child draw a safe place where the monsters cannot enter and discuss the feelings surrounding this new-found comfort. For example, in Figure 5-5 a 6-year-old boy repeatedly drew large "mother" monsters breathing fire on their "baby monsters." This drawing was indicative of this child's relationship with his mother. Because of the therapist's directive, he drew a cave under the tree where the "baby monster" would be safe.

For adolescents, groups can be more insight-oriented, as drawings become more symbolic and used for expression of internal conflict and clarification. Issues that tend to be of general importance in this age grouping include: 1) *identity confusion/formation issues,* in which possible directives might be: "Draw who you are (e.g., likes, dislikes, strengths, weaknesses, feelings); draw your mask and who is behind it; draw your world; draw your goals; how do you see yourself five years from now?"; 2) *sexual identity problems,* where it is often helpful to have all boy or all girl groups so they are not self-conscious regarding these issues and where directives might include drawings of the "ideal" boyfriend or girlfriend to encourage discussion about relationships; 3) *authority (rebellion, anger)/ independence conflicts,* in which the therapist usually allows more "free" drawings in the group.

Figure 5-6 portrays a 17-year-old male's fantasy that in five years he would be in jail. He was, at that time, very depressed. The other members of the group shared this pessimistic view with him, and an important discussion ensued which offered this particular youth more hope for his future.

In Figure 5-7, we can observe a 16-year-old's depiction of his mask(s) after the therapist instructed the group to draw their mask. It was noteworthy that he saw himself as wearing more than one mask – "mister happy," "mister bad ass," and "mister cool." This is usually indicative of youths who tend to be more manipulative, as they know how to play various roles when the situation meets their purposes.

Generally speaking, older individuals are more resistant to using drawings to express themselves than other age groups. Partly, this is due to the fact that often it has been a long time since they constructed drawings and that they may feel it is "childlike." The older individual may also be less open to change, although with encouragement this resistance can be overcome.

Figure 5-5

The therapist may ask older individuals to draw memories (both good and bad) to support the life review process (Landgarten, 1981). Often these individuals' identities are strengthened by remembering the past and graphically recording it.

In Figure 5-8 we see an 80-year-old woman's sketch of her childhood home. The shaky line quality of this particular drawing may have been a manifestation of this woman's tardive dyskinesia symptoms, which were readily apparent. As in this picture, this woman often used the color red, which was possibly indicative of the anger she was experiencing. She many times used the group to ventilate her anger concerning having to remain hospitalized. During the completion of this drawing, she verbalized many memories of her early years at home. This open discussion stimulated other group members to share their recollections.

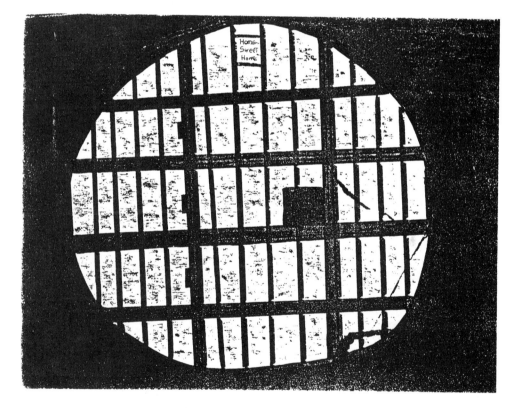

Figure 5-6

The therapist may also ask older individuals to complete drawings that tend to stimulate more open expression, such as scribbles. The therapist could also request drawings that make it easier to express the frustrations accompanying growing old (e.g., being dependent on others). Drawings constructed through the combined efforts of older individuals should emphasize worthwhile accomplishments, such as doing a drawing to be viewed by others. The therapist may even have the participants frame and display their drawings in their own show.

For older individuals, the media used for drawings is an important consideration. Finger dexterity may be limited (e.g., an arthritic older person may have difficulty applying pressure with a pencil); therefore, it may be better to use oil pastels or felt-tip pens, which transfer to paper more easily (Landgarten, 1981).

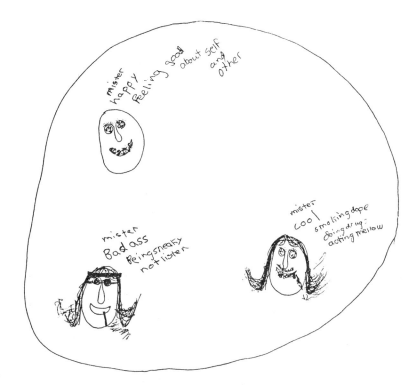

Figure 5-7

163

MY HOME

Figure 5-8

CASE ILLUSTRATION

The following case illustration demonstrates the inclusion of drawings into an ongoing outpatient adult psychotherapy group led by a psychologist and later joined by an art therapist. A block of time between $1^{1}/_{4}$ to $1^{3}/_{4}$ hours was established for each session when drawings were used as a catalyst for discussion. This provided enough time for reacting to and discussing each other's drawings when completed, since it took approximately a half hour to execute the drawings, depending on the directive provided. This extra time was also necessary for cleaning up and putting away the art supplies.

The core group consisted of six members who were 30 to 40 years of age, well-educated and sophisticated, and who were generally creative in their approach to life. The central therapeutic issues addressed in this group included problems in their respective relationships and careers. All group members also experienced symptoms of recurring depression and anxiety.

The following examples illustrate some of the relevant stages of the group process that have been outlined in this chapter.

1. Introductory Drawings

Lyn drew a cabin in the mountains where he retreated for "peace and tranquility" (Figure 5-9). The linear quality in the drawing revealed the high level of anxiety that he was experiencing during this initial phase of the group. The subject matter chosen for this particular drawing also suggested his tendency to withdraw from interpersonal contact as a means of coping with this stress. Subsequently, Lyn disclosed to the group members that he had an extensive history of alcohol abuse, which sometimes caused him to stay inside his apartment for weeks at a time.

Figure 5-9

Jim drew pictures in the way he perceived the world, "from two feet away and, at best, muddled." He indicated to the group that this interpersonal style for him had been continuing for "much too long." This particular drawing was divided in half (see Figure 5-10). The top portion for him was meant to represent the future, with the bottom portraying his past, which consisted of a severe emotional disturbance (i.e., a past diagnosis of schizophrenia). It was salient for the co-therapists to have known that Jim had been hospitalized several times in his past due to suicide attempts. This knowledge added credence to the hypothesis that the split quality of the drawing represented the possibility of borderline dependency, of which suicidal gestures are an important discriminating feature. The additional observation that his drawing lacked color also suggested underlying depression. The fact that Jim was able to recognize the confusion in his own drawing indicated that he was functioning relatively well during the initial phases of the group.

Figure 5-10

In Figure 5-11 by Hank, where he constructed a vehicle with one wheel scooping up the woods, he remarked that "now is the winter of our discontent made glorious summer by this sun of ours." This seemed to represent for him a portrait of himself as a vehicle containing knowledge with a confused sense of direction. Indeed, it was difficult to determine which way the vehicle was traveling and it also appeared to be dragging on one end. This end had an opening in the shape of a mouth, which is often thought of as an indicator of dependency conflicts. The drawing also included a house placed in the corner with a question mark, which seemed to represent his concern regarding his relationship with his wife. The difference in size between the two objects possibly suggested the importance he attached to each problem area.

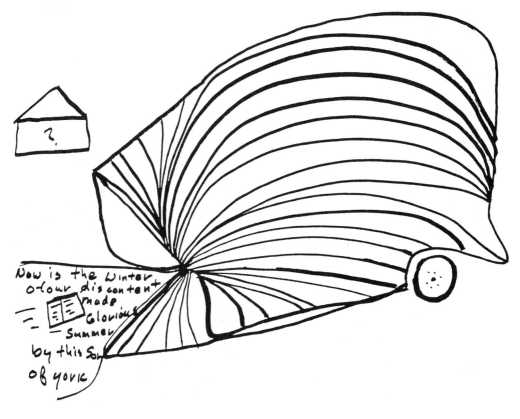

Figure 5-11

2. Drawings to Identify Problems and Goals

A directive implemented during part of the group process to aid the members in identifying their strengths and weaknesses was a request to illustrate their most "together" and "untogether" times. The following example is a product resulting from this intervening strategy.

During this session, Lois drew her most "untogether" time as this angry figure with lines exploding outward (see Figure 5-12). This picture was thought to represent her separation from an earlier boyfriend. Her most "together" time revealed a "less angry" figure contained in the shape of a mandala (see Figure 5-13). In viewing these drawings separately, one sees that even in her most troubled times she was still able to contain her anger in the diamond shape behind the figure. The group suggested to her that the ability to totally control her emotions (as portrayed in these drawings) may have been a problem for her at times, as she possessed a tendency to withold the full expression of her true feelings.

Another directive added during this phase of the group was to ask the members to draw their dominant "issue" and/or "feeling." Outcomes from these drawings tended to reveal each member's central underlying conflict. For example, Hank drew his dominant issue as a strong man standing on a

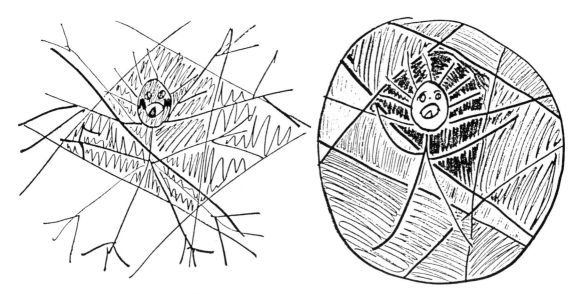

Figure 5-12   Figure 5-13

168

ledge pushing another (weaker) man into a mouthlike shape that Hank described as a trampoline (Figure 5-14).

The trampoline was supposed to represent for Hank his ability to recover (or bounce back) from any emotional setback. However, the group suggested to him that the trampoline did not give him much control. Here again the drawing provides concrete evidence of his underlying lack of control, although his verbal presentation tried to underplay these feelings by offering the positive attribute of "bouncing back."

Hank also included in the drawing the statement, "People in positions of authority are dumb." It was evident in these faceless figures that Hank lacked a clear sense of identity; they also revealed his then present feelings of helplessness and anger after being fired from a job.

Another member of the group, Nadia, elaborated on this directive by drawing her then "dominant feeling," which was exemplified by a portrait of herself standing on a cliff entitled "distraught" (see Figure 5-15). In a drawing such as this, the clinician must be alert for suicidal ideation and explore with the person whether or not he/she has been feeling depressed enough to harm him/herself.

Another drawing directive given to the group, which offered the members a format by which to identify their problem areas, conflicts, and goals,

Figure 5-14

169

was the suggestion to draw either their "problem and solution" or their "past and future" in relation to their problems.

Jim's drawing of his "problem and solution" was integrated into a sketch of a sculpture (see Figure 5-16). Within the base of the drawing is a self-portrait with a question mark, which signified his personal state of turmoil. The column containing a dollar sign was his attempt at symbolically representing a solution. The ball shape on the top represented the "lifestyle" he ultimately desired. He added to this drawing symbols in the foundation and steps on the side to figuratively help him to reach the column. The overall drawing was symmetrical, which was viewed as a sign of an integrated personality. Yet the top of the columns appeared unattainable, which probably revealed his underlying feelings of impotence.

In Lyn's attempt at a "past and future" drawing, he indicated that his past was unidirectional, which was unsatisfactory and possibly maladaptive for him (see Figure 5-17). He drew his future going in all directions taking care of all aspects of his life, which was a more satisfying state for him. This shape had the appearance of an explosion which suggested the possibility of anger, an area which the art therapist explored when the group shared their work.

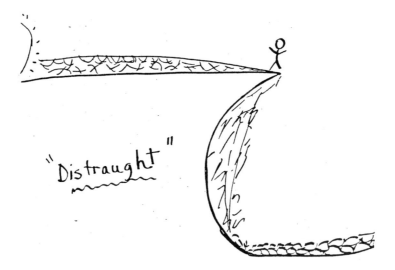

Figure 5-15

170

Figure 5-16

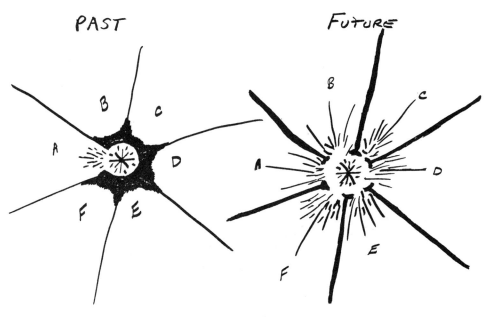

Figure 5-17

3. Drawings to Increase Interaction and to Build Cohesiveness

Drawings distributed among the group members were generally helpful in building group cohesion (see Figure 5-18). Each member started a drawing and passed it on for other group members to make additions. Only when it returned to the beginning person was it titled. It is important to mention that in these kinds of "pass around" drawings each group member has a different color for identification purposes. The drawing seen here was representative of this process. The title to this particular drawing led group members into a confrontation with the psychologist co-leader regarding their feelings that she was abandoning them to go on vacation. When sharing their drawings, they revealed that they were particularly anxious about being left alone with the art therapist co-leader who required drawings. This led into a very helpful discussion of their fear of revealing too much of themselves unknowingly in their drawings to the newer and less familiar therapist.

However, another attempt at a shared drawing portrayed this group's capacity for support (see Figure 5-19). Nadia, who initiated this drawing,

Figure 5-18

drew the cloud to stand for her feelings of sadness. Subsequently, other group members added the sun coming from behind the cloud, a friendly plane, and the wind "protecting with its arms and trying to break up the cloud by blowing on it." The initiator of the drawing was receptive to this support by titling the picture "security and warmth." (It is important to note that prior to this drawing, this particular member was isolated and withdrawn.)

CONCLUDING REMARKS

This group continued for another year with only intermittent breaks. Each of the group members gained a sense of intimacy and security that they had not experienced before the beginning of the group. With this therapeutic support, each member was able to approach his/her respective life with a greater sense of direction and purpose.

The members were able to make use of their drawings effectively to

Figure 5-19

173

focus on specific problem areas and keep a concrete record of their progress. The drawings added a richness to the ending of the group as they stimulated many unique remembrances and asssociations. For many of these individuals, the drawings provided a platform to face and confront extremely emotional issues that they were previously having a difficult time verbalizing. The drawings brought these emotionally-laden issues to the forefront so that therapeutic help could be provided.

Appendix

ANNOTATED BIBLIOGRAPHY

Bolander, K. *Assessing personality through tree drawings.* New York: Basic Books, 1977.

This comprehensive book is for the serious student of projective techniques and of tree drawings in particular. Its contents include a thorough history of the origins and development of Bolander's interpretive methods as well as insightful comparisons to other scoring systems. The book discusses the various details of tree drawings and their possible interpretations, including such aspects as positioning, size, direction, types, parts, ground, and knotholes. Case illustrations and tree drawing reproductions support the author's perspective.

Betensky, M. *Self-discovery through self-expression.* Springfield, IL: Charles C Thomas, 1973.

Generally, this text is broad in scope and theoretical orientation with its contents derived from psychology, art therapy, sociology, and anthropology. Part one consists of 10 studies of art therapy used with children and adolescents. Part two presents essays on various factors of art therapy, including art used to elicit self-expression, the use of color, roles of art and play, and issues of transference.

DiLeo, J.H. *Interpreting children's drawings*. New York: Brunner/Mazel, 1983.

This comprehensive volume is an extension of Dr. DiLeo's earlier book, *Children's Drawings as Diagnostic Aids*. The author provides much interpretive material for his many examples but also warns of overinterpretation and attempts to answer many questions relating to resistance and developmental levels. Additional material treated in this book are such topics as changing sex roles, effects of family pathology, and laterality.

Feder, E., & Feder, F. *The expressive arts therapies: Art, music and dance as psychotherapy*. Englewood Cliffs, NJ: Prentice-Hall, 1981.

This book provides an integrated overview of the various theoretical models underlying the therapies that use the arts as their primary focus. The authors blend the diagnostic and treatment process into explanations of how each of these types of therapists bring their clinical skills and tools into their respective trade. Through many case illustrations and explanations the authors attempt to vividly describe what expressive therapists actually do.

Fleshman, B., & Fryrear, J.L. *The arts in therapy*. Chicago: Nelson-Hall, 1981.

This book provides an overview of the arts in therapy. After presenting a general background, the authors detail the modalities of psychodrama, music, visual arts, movement, drama, poetry and storytelling, and photography and film. This book is an excellent introduction for those clinicians who are not familiar with the possibilities and uses of creative services within the mental health profession.

Gardner, H. *Artful scribbles: The significance of children's drawings*. New York: Basic Books, 1980.

Gardner observes the development of children through their artwork. His philosophical perspective challenges many of the previous thoughts on the developing child, and he considers both aesthetic processes and art products in this provocative book.

Hammer, E. (Ed.). *The clinical application of projective drawings*. Springfield, IL: Charles C Thomas, 1958.

A pioneering book in drawing techniques. Dr. Hammer brought together the leading figures of this time in one extraordinary reference volume. The book describes a variety of drawing procedures helpful as tools for the diagnostician. Theory and many clinical vignettes of the D-A-P and H-T-P make this a classic contribution to the field.

176

Kellogg, R. *Analyzing children's art*. Palo Alto, CA: Mayfield, 1970.

This book describes the mental development of the child that occurs through his/ her working in art. It provides a glimpse into the author's research, in which she has collected and catalogued a million drawings completed by young children. It extends her earlier work, *What Children Scribble and Why*, by presenting the analysis of children's drawings to 8 years of age.

Koppitz, E.M. *Psychological evaluation of children's human figure drawings*. New York: Grune & Stratton, 1968.

In this classic text, Koppitz presents human figure drawings of children ages 5 to 12 for analysis and scoring both as a developmental test of mental maturity and as a projective test of underlying needs and conflicts. Koppitz developed scoring systems for these two approaches after standardizing them on drawings from over 1800 public school children. Chapters are also included on the use of family drawings and on the use of figure drawings to assess school readiness and to diagnose brain trauma.

Kramer, E. *Art as therapy with children*. New York: Schocken Books, 1971.

The focus of this book is on using art as therapy (not as merely a tool within the psychotherapeutic experience). It emphasizes such issues as ambivalence, identity conflicts, aggression, defenses, and sublimation. Most of this book, by one of art therapy's pioneers, depends on clinical vignettes and longer case histories.

Kwiatkowska, H. Y. *Family therapy and evaluation through art*. Springfield, IL: Charles C Thomas, 1978.

This book describes the special kind of communication provided by graphic and plastic media used with families in therapy. Kwiatkowska presents her pioneering work in family art evaluations through examples of hysterical and schizophrenic families. Also offered are family art techniques used as research tools and differentiating between family art therapy when used adjunctively and when used as the primary modality in treatment.

Landgarten, H.B. *Clinical art therapy: A comprehensive guide*. New York: Brunner/Mazel, 1981.

True to its title, this book attempts to provide a complete text and reference source for the discipline of clinical art therapy. The book contains numerous practical guidelines and offers advice on using various media in different settings. Heavily illustrated, this book considers aspects of family art psychotherapy, latency-age children, adolescents, adults, and the aged, and rehabilitation and treatment of chronic pain.

Lyddiatt, E.M. *Spontaneous painting and modeling: A practical approach to therapy.* New York: St.Martin's Press, 1971.

This is a practical book on establishing art programs in psychiatric hospitals, which emphasizes the sublimation process involved in spontaneous painting and modeling in clay. It is based on the author's vast experiences with psychiatric patients and is grounded in the theory and teachings of C.G. Jung. The book demonstrates in everyday terms what occurs when Jung's concepts are used as the foundation for daily work with mentally ill individuals.

Maynard, F. *Guiding your child to a more creative life.* New York: Doubleday, 1973.

Unlike the other books listed in this section, this one is written primarily for parents. Although for the lay market, the suggestions and "recipes" for using the medium of art are basically adaptable to health and mental health professions. This book additionally includes references for many "how-to" guides in utilizing art with children.

Oaklander, V. *Windows to our children: A gestalt therapy approach to children and adolescents.* Moab, UT: Real People Press, 1978.

This book describes Dr. Oaklander's personal experiences in working with children and it presents the children speaking of themselves. It describes the use of various techniques within Dr. Oaklander's philosophical framework. Chapters on "Drawing and Fantasy," "Storytelling, Poetry and Puppets," "Sensory Experience," and "Specific Problem Behaviors" make this a very intriguing and practical book.

Paras Kevas, C. *A structural approach to art therapy methods.* Elmsford, NY: Collegium, 1979.

This book was written as a basic introduction to the field of art therapy. It begins by defining art therapy, then offers four philosophical viewpoints within the field. It also attempts to differentiate between art therapy as a separate discipline and art education. The final portion of the book focuses on using art in groups with many practical suggestions.

Robbins, A., & Sibley, L. B. *Creative art therapy.* New York: Brunner/Mazel, 1976.

This is an introductory text which details the approaches of various art therapies. The book emphasizes the necessity for the training of an art therapist to function as a facilitator as well as a clinical interviewer. Issues that are discussed include ego development, respect for the client, creative growth, meaning of productions, and communicating information. Case studies in different settings are presented.

Silver, R. *Developing cognitive and creative skills through art*. Baltimore: University Park Press, 1978.

This book details a variety of programs and methods one can use when working with handicapped children. The emphasis is on using these tools with children who are limited by communication disorders, learning disabilities, and hearing impairment. The book also offers descriptions of the uses of art in assessment and explains the development of artistic skills through examples of drawing and other media.

Wadeson, H. *Art psychotherapy*. New York: John Wiley & Sons, 1980.

This attempt at a definitive text offers the reader sections on the history, philosophy, and fundamentals of art therapy in addition to how art therapy can be used to evaluate and treat affective illness, schizophrenia, neurosis, and addiction. It also provides chapters on group and family art therapy and examines the problems encountered when trying to do research in this field. An appendix with useful techniques for providing general subjects for pictures, loosening up ideas, and family and group exercises make this a most complete volume.

SUGGESTED JOURNALS

Art Therapy. American Art Therapy Association, Mundelein, IL.

This quarterly journal is the official journal of the American Art Therapy Association. It provides feature articles on the process of art therapy and its associated theory and professional issues. It also offers the subscriber such things as readers' comments, a job exchange board, and recent reviews of the literature, both of books and articles.

The American Journal of Art Therapy. Vermont College of Norwich University, Montpelier, VT.

Originally the *Bulletin of Art Therapy*. This is the oldest art therapy journal. It focuses on art education, rehabilitation, and psychotherapy.

Journal of the National Art Education Association. Reston, VA.

This bimonthly journal is the official document of the National Art Education Association. Its readership is offered a variety of articles related to art education.

The Arts in Psychotherapy: An International Journal. Fayetteville, N.Y.

A quarterly journal for individuals in the health and mental health and education disciplines. Its international focus highlights art, dance, drama, music, and poetry used in the practice of assessment and therapy.

References

Anastasi, A. *Psychological testing* (5th ed.). New York: Macmillan, 1982.

Appel, K. E. Drawings by children as aids in personality studies. *American Journal of Orthopsychiatry*, 1931, *1*, 129-144.

Axline, V. M. *Play therapy* (rev. ed.). Boston: Houghton Mifflin, 1969.

Bateson, G. *Steps to an ecology of mind*. New York: Ballantine Books, 1972.

Bender, L. *A visual motor gestalt test and its clinical use*. New York: The American Orthopsychiatric Association, 1938.

Betensky, M. *Self-discovery through self-expression*. Springfield, IL: Charles C Thomas, 1973.

Bolander, K. *Assessing personality through tree drawings*. New York: Basic Books, 1977.

Buck, J. N. The H-T-P test. *Journal of Clinical Psychology*, 1948, *4*, 151-159.

Burns, R. C., & Kaufman, S. H. *Kinetic family drawings (K-F-D): An introduction to understanding children through kinetic drawing*. New York: Brunner/Mazel, 1970.

Burt, C. *Mental and scholastic tests*. London: P. S. King and Son, 1921.

Cane, F. *The artist in each of us*. New York: Pantheon, 1951.

Caplan, G. *Principles of preventive psychiatry*. New York: Basic Books, 1964.

Cardone, L., Marengo, J., & Calisch, A. Conjoint use of art and verbal techniques for the intensification of the psychotherapeutic group experience. *The Arts in Psychotherapy*, 1982, *9*(4), 263-268.

Corey, G. *Theory and practice of group counseling*. Monterey, CA: Brooks/Cole, 1981.

DiLeo, J. H. *Interpreting children's drawings*. New York: Brunner/Mazel, 1983.

Feder, E., & Feder, B. *The expressive arts therapies: Art, music & dance as psychotherapy*. Englewood Cliffs, NJ: Prentice-Hall, 1981.

Fleshman, B., & Fryrear, J. L. *The arts in therapy*. Chicago: Nelson-Hall, 1981.

Frank, L. K. *Projective methods*. Springfield, IL: Charles C Thomas, 1948.

Freud, S. *New introductory lectures on psychoanalysis*. New York: Norton, 1933.

Freud, S. *The interpretation of dreams*. New York: Basic Books, 1958. (originally published in 1900).

Gabel, S. The draw a story game: An aid in understanding and working with children. *The Arts in Psychotherapy*, 1984, *11*, 187-196.

Gardner, R. A. *Psychotherapeutic approaches to the resistant child*. New York: Jason Aronson, 1975.

Goodenough, F. L. *Measurement of intelligence by drawings*. New York: Harcourt, Brace & World, 1926.

Gumaer, J. *Counseling and therapy for children*. New York: Macmillan, 1984.

Haley, J. *Strategies of psychotherapy*. New York: Grune & Stratton, 1963.

Haley, J. *Problem-solving therapy*. San Francisco: Jossey-Bass, 1976.

Haley, J. *Leaving home: The therapy of disturbed young people*. New York: McGraw-Hill, 1980.

Hammer, E. F. *Clinical applications of projective drawings*. Springfield, IL: Charles C Thomas, 1967.

Harris, D. B. *Children's drawings as measures of intellectual maturity*. New York: Harcourt, Brace, & World, 1963.

Hathaway, S. R., & Meehl, P. E. *An atlas for the clinical use of the MMPI*. Minneapolis: University of Minnesota Press, 1951.

Jastak, J. F., & Jastak, S. *The Wide Range Achievement Test* (rev. ed.). Wilmington, DE: Jastak Associates, 1978.

Jolles, I. *A catalog for the qualitative interpretation of the H-T-P*. Los Angeles: Western Psychological Services, 1971.

Jung, C. G. *The portable Jung*. (Ed. by J. Campbell. Translated by R. F. C. Hull). New York: Viking Press, 1971.

Kellogg, R. *Analyzing children's art*. Palo Alto: Mayfield Publishing, 1970.

Koch, K. *The tree test: The tree-drawing test as an aid in psychodiagnosis*. (2nd ed.) (English translation). Bern: Hans Huber, 1952.

Koppitz, E. M. *Psychological evaluation of children's human figure drawings*. New York: Grune & Stratton, 1968.

Koppitz, E. M. *Psychological evaluation of human figure drawings by middle school pupils*. New York: Grune & Stratton, 1984.

Kramer, E. *Art as therapy with children*. New York: Schocken Books, 1971.

Kris, E. *Psychoanalytic exploration in art*. New York: International Universities Press, 1952.

Kwiatkowska, H. Y. *Family therapy and evaluation through art*. Springfield, IL: Charles C Thomas, 1978.

Landgarten, H. B. *Clinical art therapy: A comprehensive guide*. New York: Brunner/Mazel, 1981.

Lindemann,E. Symptomatology and management of acute grief. *American Journal of Psychiatry*, 1944, *101*, 141-148.

Lyddiatt, E. M. *Spontaneous painting and modeling: A practical approach in therapy*. New York: St. Martin's Press, 1971.

Machover, K. *Personality projection in the drawing of the human figure*. Springfield, IL: Charles C Thomas, 1952.

Madanes, C. *Strategic family therapy*. San Francisco: Jossey-Bass, 1981.

Minuchin, S. *Families and family therapy*. Cambridge, MA: Harvard University Press, 1974.

Minuchin, S., & Fishman, C. *Family therapy techniques*. Cambridge, MA: Harvard University Press, 1981.

Murray, H. A. *Thematic Apperception Test.* Cambridge, MA: Harvard University Press, 1943.

Naumburg, M. *Dynamically oriented art therapy: Its principles and practice.* New York: Grune & Stratton, 1966.

Oaklander, V. *Windows to our children.* Moab, UT: Real People Press, 1978.

Palmer, J. O. *The psychological assessment of children.* New York: Wiley, 1970.

Rhyne, J. *The gestalt art experience.* Monterey, CA: Brooks/Cole, 1973.

Robbins, A., & Sibley, L. B. *Creative art therapy.* New York: Brunner/Mazel, 1976.

Rogers, C. *On becoming a person.* Boston: Houghton-Mifflin, 1961.

Rorschach, H. *Psychodiagnostics.* Bern: Verlag Hans Huber, 1942.

Rubin, J. A. *Child art therapy.* New York: Van Nostrand Reinhold, 1978.

Satir, V. *Conjoint family therapy* (rev. ed.). Palo Alto: Science and Behavior Books, 1967.

Schutz, W. On group composition. *Journal of Abnormal and Social Psychology,* 1961, *62,* 275-281.

Sobol, B. Art therapy and strategic family therapy. *American Journal of Art Therapy,* 1982, *21,* 23-31.

Stone, B. Group art therapy with mothers of autistic children. *The Arts in Psychotherapy,* 1982, *9,* 31-48.

Wadeson, H. *Art psychotherapy.* New York: Wiley, 1980.

Wechsler, D. *Manual for the Wechsler Adult Intelligence Scale-Revised.* New York: Psychological Corporation, 1981.

Winnicott, D. W. *Therapeutic consultations in child psychiatry.* London: Hogarth Press, 1971.

Wolff, W. Projective methods for personality analysis of expressive behavior in preschool children. *Character & Personality,* 1942, *10,* 309-330.

Yalom I. D. *The theory and practice of group psychotherapy.* New York: Basic Books, 1970.

Index

187

189